MY LIFE AS A TEACHER

◆◆◆

By the Author of

◆◆◆

THE MEMORY OF CERTAIN PERSONS

WHAT IS MUSIC?

THE VOYAGE OF CAPTAIN BART

MRS. DORATT

CASANOVA'S WOMEN

GIVE ME LIBERTY

THE START OF THE ROAD

ETC.

MY LIFE

AS A TEACHER

◆◆◆

by

John Erskine

J. B. LIPPINCOTT COMPANY

PHILADELPHIA AND NEW YORK

NOTE

❖❖❖

WHEN I wrote *The Memory of Certain Persons* I could not find room in one volume for all the valued friendships of a lifetime, nor for the comment I wished to make on my three careers, in education, in music, and in writing.

This volume is intended to supplement the outline of my work as a teacher which I gave in *The Memory*. When reference to that work is necessary I shall use the shortened title.

I did my teaching at Amherst, at Columbia, at Beaune, and on numerous lecture trips. For convenience I shall here treat these phases of my experience as though they were separate and distinct, though there were two instalments of the Amherst and Columbia chapters, and the public lecturing accompanied and overlapped all the other activities, both at home and abroad. The chronology is given correctly in *The Memory*. The reader will not be confused by a slight regrouping of incidents.

The material in Chapter XIII, on the Ph.D. degree, appeared in the *New York Times* for June 3, 1945. Chapter XI, on National Training, was first published in the *Review of Reviews* for October, 1919. I thank both publications for permission to reprint.

J. E.

CONTENTS

❖❖❖

MY LIFE AS A TEACHER

◆◆◆

CHAPTER I

Definitions

NOTHING in education needs explaining more than this, that a teacher may be neither a professor nor an educator, that a professor may mature to the age of retirement without teaching or educating, and that an educator, without loss of reputation, may profess nothing, and never face a class.

A teacher is one who shows his fellow man how to do something, who imparts an active skill, and who kindles the desire to acquire this skill and to use it. In all creatures there is a natural ambition to live, which necessarily includes an ambition to learn, but even a natural ambition will need encouragement. The cow teaches the newborn calf to walk, the mother bird teaches her young to fly, though neither cow nor bird, so far as we know, has a teacher's diploma, or the equivalent, from a normal school. If the calf is reluctant to stand up, the cow gets behind and under, and gives a dramatic boost. If the fledgling recoils from the unsolid air, the mother bird pushes it overboard. This is teaching, of no mean sort.

A professor is a person who knows all about a subject, or professes to know all about it, or at least a good deal about it, or about a part of it. If the part he knows is a very small part, the professor is called a specialist. When a sufficient number of specialists are assembled on a college faculty, the subject of which each knows only a small part is said to be covered, and the academic department to which they all belong is regarded as fully manned. In ancient Ireland, if legend may be trusted, there was a tower so high that it took two persons to see to the top of it. One would begin at the bottom and look up as far as sight could reach, the other would begin where the first left off, and see the rest of the way.

I would not imply that no professor is a good teacher, but I do say plainly that professors are not necessarily teachers; they are not trained to be, colleges and universities do not engage them as such. A professor wears his Ph.D. to show not that he can teach, but that as a reservoir of knowledge he is reasonably full.

Scholarship is not judged by its usefulness; it is supposed to imply other and superior qualities. A scholar is honored for his industry, for his thoroughness, and for the correctness of his methods. Whether his fellow men wish to acquire or share any of the knowledge stored up in him, is an irrelevant question. In fact, whenever scholarship is applied with success to the amelioration of life, it risks the reputation of being tarnished; it is no longer "pure."

If a university can afford to maintain not only a staff of professors, those who know, but also a staff of junior instructors who can teach, the inarticulate elders are more highly honored and receive the big salaries. A professor does no harm to his reputation, he may even improve it, by saying and writing nothing. The patina of silence is admired by connoisseurs. It is not to Oxford dons exclusively that George Santayana's mordant remark applies: "The thoughts of these men are like the sybiline leaves, profound but lost."

Educators are those who plan the work of teachers, or make possible a scholarly career. College presidents are educators, so are college trustees, so was Andrew Carnegie, so was Cecil Rhodes. Just as a scholar may still be a scholar, even though his knowledge is unused or unusable, so an educator retains the reputation of an educator even though the program he invents is lop-sided or prejudiced.

James Russell Lowell, speaking in 1886 at the two hundred and fiftieth anniversary of the founding of Harvard University, quoted from a letter written by John Winthrop, Jr. in 1663 to an English friend: "I make bold to send here inclosed a kind of rarity. . . . It is two papers of Latin composed by two Indians now scollars in the Colledge in this country, and the writing is with their own hands. . . . Possibly as a novelty of that kind it may be acceptable, being a reall fruit of that hopeful worke yt is begun amongst them . . . testifying thus much that I received them of those Indians out of their own hands, and had ready answers from them to many questions I propounded to them in yt language, and heard them both express several sentences in Greeke also."

From this passage it may be concluded that in primitive Harvard the art of teaching was further advanced than the philosophy of education. One of these Indians was graduated and received his diploma. The other, having learned to write Latin, went back to the woods. It is not recorded that the one who took his degree ever appeared at a class reunion. Perhaps his feelings were hurt. Perhaps he expected his clever Latin teachers to reciprocate by mastering his American tongue, but they seem to have been indifferent, even as to the correct pronunciation of his name.

With these definitions I can now tell my story. For most of my life my temperament and my occupation was that of a teacher, but now and then I have been quite scholarly, and at moments I have played the part of an educator, more often than not on a large stage. But I liked teaching best. The teacher deals directly with youth, and I love youth. The teacher, through his pupils, may influence the future, which is perhaps the part of time which most deserves our attention.

CHAPTER II

I Am Invited to Teach

M Y CAREER as a teacher began, or was at the point of beginning, when I received a curiously scrawled note from the President's office, Amherst College, Amherst, Massachusetts. The note was dated April 13, 1903, and addressed to John Erskine, Esq.

> My dear Sir
>
> I have inquired of Professor Trent respect'n'g a teacher of English and he has recommended you—I am to be in New York Thursd'y evening and Friday. If convenient to you, I shall be glad to meet you at the Manhattan hotel at 9 to 9.30 Friday morning. Will you be so good as to write whether you will see me then or not.
>
> Yours resp'tf'ly,
> GUY HARRIS

The signature, in contrast to the rest of the note, was clear; beyond question it was Guy Harris. But a fellow student at Columbia thought the President of Amherst was named George. In the University Library I consulted the Amherst catalog. My fellow student was right.

The Manhattan Hotel stood at Madison Avenue and Forty-second Street, in the space now occupied by the National City Bank.

Shortly after nine on Friday morning I appeared in the lobby. With extraordinary vividness I remember that my suit was well pressed and my hair had been cut the day before. To the best of my ability I was collaborating with Fate. Naturally my hopeful mood was dashed when the room clerk, answering my inquiry for Dr. George Harris, told me he had never heard of the gentleman. Nor of Guy Harris. There were plenty of Harrises on the register but no Guys or Georges.

At twenty minutes to ten a short, distinguished-looking man approached the desk. He wore a gray business suit, quite as well-pressed as mine. His gray hair was parted in the middle, there was gray in his moustache. He had a large, curving nose which even before he spoke suggested a Maine accent. He walked with a long stride, and his head was thrust down and forward, as though to butt or charge.

"Anyone here asking for Harris?"

It *was* a Maine voice.

I stepped forward, President Harris extended a large, soft and cordial hand, and we walked toward the hotel parlor, the windows of which looked on Madison Avenue.

"Waiting for me long?"

"The hotel hadn't your name."

He laughed, a friendly snort. "Perhaps they have it under *N* for Norris. They frequently do."

We found two chairs at a window, on the identical spot, I should say, where the bank manager now sits at his desk. With no loss of time the President asked where I was born, what church I belonged to, was I married, and did I have my Ph.D.

When I said I was an Episcopalian he remarked that he had once thought of being an Episcopalian himself, but having started life as a Congregationalist he had become used to that condition. He showed satisfaction or relief when I told him the label or certificate of scholarship would be affixed to me in June. He seemed relieved also that I was not yet married. I noted with some regret that he hadn't the slightest curiosity about my thesis subject.

As to my teaching, he said an instructor was needed for the freshman English class, for the whole class. He rather feared the freshmen might be difficult at first, since Professor Genung, my predecessor, a fine gentleman but a trifle soft, had permitted the tradition to grow up that freshmen should do no work in English, not even write an essay.

I asked what would become of Professor Genung; was he leaving the campus? Retiring, perhaps? Oh, no, the College would continue to benefit by Professor Genung's immense scholarship. He would withdraw from freshman English, and offer a course for seniors in the Book of Job. Was I acquainted with Professor Genung's book on Job? He was something of a specialist; few men in the United States knew more about Job.

Dr. Harris closed the interview by confiding, apparently as an after-thought, that my salary would be either $1,000 or $1,200, he couldn't say which. It would probably be a good idea to visit Amherst one of these pleasant spring days and find myself a place to room and board.

Since I have already described President Harris at length,[1] I speak of him here only to illustrate my definitions. He was neither a teacher nor a scholar, and as I gathered correctly from our first meeting, he was not an executive. He never made clear what he expected me to accomplish; I doubt if he knew. Had he known, he would have mentioned it. Had he been dissatisfied with me, he would have mentioned that too. Whatever dream, or plan, or hope he cherished for his college, he forgot to tell his faculty. He was not an educator. He was a very kind gentleman, a retired minister. He still preached on occasion, but not enough to interrupt his presidency, which was the form retirement took with him. When he engaged me, I think he got a good teacher, but it was nothing but

[1] *The Memory*, p. 141.

luck; he didn't know then whether I was good or bad, and neither did I.

Ten days or so after meeting Dr. Harris, I had a letter from Chancellor Frank Strong of the University of Kansas, at Lawrence. The letter was dated April 27, 1903. It was typewritten; not a word in it was illegible, not a sentence vague. Evidently it came from a man who knew his mind, and could say where he wished to go.

Mr. John Erskine
  306 West 93rd Street
    New York City

My dear Sir:

Your name has been suggested to me for the position of associate professor of English literature of this University. The position is a new one and will pay $1500 a year. Living expenses are not high in Lawrence so that salary represents considerably more than it would in New York City. There is a reasonable chance for advancement as the funds of the Board of Regents and the interests of the University allow, and the position is important enough, we believe, to merit the attention of a first class man. The University is growing and already is one of the best equipped in the West. I understand that you are considering another place and it may be that you have already decided. I should like to know at once whether you care to look this way. What I have heard about you makes me feel that I should be glad to give your application careful consideration.

With best wishes, I am
Very truly yours,
FRANK STRONG
Chancellor

I was attracted to the West and I liked the Chancellor's letter. The difference in salary seemed insignificant, since it would go into train fare whenever I came home to New York. Having committed myself to Amherst, I disliked to back out, and perhaps no other place would prove a happier opportunity. But if I had gone to Kansas, I believe I should have stayed in the West, which is still a brave new world, and will be·so for decades.

Seventeen years later I had a second opportunity to cast in my lot with the University of Kansas. When Chancellor Strong retired in 1920, the Board of Regents and the Governor of the State, Henry J. Allen, invited me to succeed him. In many ways the opportunity was immense, but it was easier to decline the chancellorship than it had been the assistant professorship. The Regents and Governor Allen asked me because of my experience at the A.E.F. University at Beaune; [2] but there I had been an educator, not a teacher, and if I accepted the chancellorship, I should have to keep on as an educator for the rest of my life. I wanted to be a teacher and I wanted to write. I told Governor Allen so in a letter dated April 30, 1920.

The invitation which your state has offered me is, I am sure, the most attractive I shall ever receive to leave my present work. I am fully conscious of the opportunity that lies ready for the right man, and of the kindly cooperation on your part which will make his task a happy one. Monday evening I was indeed almost swept out of my life-long ambition to do service as teacher and writer. In these intervening days, however, as I wrote Dr. Mason,[3] I have been realizing that there must be many men of greater ability than mine who could go to Kansas without the regrets that I should undoubtedly feel at giving up a work which is the first choice of my affections.

[2] *The Memory,* pp. 311-37.
[3] Wilbur N. Mason, Board of Administration, Kansas University.

CHAPTER III

I Begin to Teach and Learn

1

WHEN President Harris talked with me at the Manhattan Hotel, I suppose he asked all the questions he thought necessary. But I wonder now why he did not ask why I wanted to teach. No other question is so searching, and none draws more startling replies. In later years, when I was interviewing candidates for a vacant instructorship, I heard one youth say he wished to teach because a quiet life appealed to him and he doubted if it could be found in the world of business. Another explained that academic society seemed attractive, at least from the outside. Since I had long been on the inside, he invited me to confirm or correct his impression. But in any case he assured me that teaching was the work he was born to do. The summer vacation offered opportunity for travel such as only lawyers and judges enjoy, and he feared he hadn't enough brains to be a lawyer.

If President Harris had asked me why I wished to teach, I should have said that I loved literature and enjoyed talking about it to anyone who would listen. I also liked to write, and would probably enjoy showing others how to do it, but at that time the teaching of composition seemed far less attractive than lecturing about great books.

I assumed that literature should be taught as I had seen Wood-berry [1] do it, by stimulating lectures which would create in the hearers a passionate love of the best authors. I assumed that the best authors would always be English poets and prose writers, and that in time I should give courses closely following the schedule which Professor Childs had established at Harvard, and which Professor Kittredge had continued after him. English literature as I defined it began with Chaucer. Of course there was a mass of Anglo-Saxon material through which Professor Price and Professor George Philip Krapp at Columbia had guided my unenthusiastic steps; there was also a mass of Middle English dreariness between the Anglo-Saxon period and Chaucer, but with Chaucer English literature came alive —only to go to sleep again until the latter days of Henry VIII. Then came the Elizabethan period, then the seventeenth century, then what I considered a polite waste of time until the close of the eighteenth century when the Romantic period began to disclose itself in Robert Burns and William Blake. The nineteenth century, naturally, divided itself into the early section, made glorious by Byron, Shelley, Keats, and Walter Scott, and the later, or Victorian, period which included Dickens and Thackeray, Tennyson and Browning, Carlyle and Ruskin, John Henry Newman, Matthew Arnold, and Water Pater. English literature stopped for me in 1892 with the death of Tennyson. When I went to Amherst in the autumn of 1903, I had seen no college catalog which offered courses in later British writers. Of course I knew George Meredith, Thomas Hardy, Algernon Swinburne, Oscar Wilde, and Rudyard Kipling, but they were all still alive, and for that reason it was impossible as yet to determine the quality of their work. To be great, a writer must be dead.

I expected to teach composition by Professor Carpenter's [2] methods, supplemented by certain things I had learned from Woodberry. More than once in college I showed him my poems and essays, my

---

[1] *The Memory*, pp. 90-95.
[2] *The Memory*, pp. 97-98.

personal and non-academic writing. I recalled how much he had taught me about punctuation, the ordinary rules of which he held in contempt, but the larger purpose of which he helped me to understand. Punctuation is helpful on a first reading; any device which makes the meaning clearer and easier to get at, is a good thing. I recalled also, and hoped to imitate in my dealings with pupils, Woodberry's inspiring assumption that I took seriously whatever I wrote and would spare no pains to improve it.

Perhaps I should supplement this account of my earliest ideals in teaching literature by saying that in 1903 I had no doubt that a somewhat exclusive love of English literature was desirable in every American student. I loved Greek literature, and French, and Italian, and I was already beginning to suspect the enormous value of Spanish literature. But it had not yet occurred to me that American boys in general needed to broaden their minds in these directions. The blindness which now seems to me most shocking was my indifference at that time to American literature. I hadn't the slightest ambition to teach it. In respectable English departments at the beginning of the twentieth century, American literature was considered an inferior subject. To give a course in it was an opportunity hardly more inviting than the privilege of correcting freshman themes.

In my first Amherst years freshman themes were the only compositions I corrected. In all colleges then, as almost to the same extent now, the freshman English course was expected to impart elementary correctness and little more. Of course the elements should have been acquired in school, but they weren't. A large proportion of my first Amherst freshmen were unable to spell. Some of them were the most remarkable *mis*spellers I have ever met. At first I was discouraged and not a little disgusted with the job I had taken on, perhaps for life, but gradually adjusting my high expectations to the stubborn facts, I instituted a spelling class for the benefit of the near-illiterate. After all, why shouldn't I teach these boys how to spell if that was what they needed to learn? Perhaps they had never enjoyed sound instruction in this fairly simple subject. Most of them,

I knew, owned a dictionary, usually a collegiate edition of Webster, but not one of them had ever glanced at the prefatory material in that reference work. They did not know that the dictionary tells the reader in advance the rules by which the words are spelled. In fact, I was moved to organize a spelling class by a remark of one of the boys that English spelling was hard because it was guided by no rules whatever.

In the course of a month or two I taught the boys to spell—at least some of them; not to spell by memory but to memorize the rules and to apply them where they were needed. By much the same method they learned to punctuate and to paragraph. By the end of the year I flattered myself that they could write with reasonable precision and clearness, marshaling their thoughts in a sensible order, and putting their sentences in an intelligent sequence. Perhaps I was justified in thinking I had done rather well; at least I had done all that my youth and inexperience permitted. But twenty years later I looked back at that freshman course at Amherst with anything but pride. I should have made the composition course for every student a personal experience, an opporunity to discover himself. Instead, I asked of them mere correctness of the conventional or academic kind, and I praised them when they gave it to me. This was all very well, but I wish I had seized every occasion for praising them when their personality slipped into their work so that they, and no one else, spoke from the page. Later at Columbia I did learn to develop writers by encouraging each individual to discover for himself the manner and the style which was natural and characteristic, but in my Amherst classes I am afraid I depended on the handwriting or the signature to let me know who wrote the theme.

Even at Amherst, however, I had exceptional moments when rare students almost taught me how to teach them. I recall vividly one morning when Talbot F. Hamlin, now a scholarly architect, read to the class a remarkable story. I knew that Talbot was more sensitive and imaginative than most boys of his age, but as he began to read I found myself under the spell of a genuine *tour de force*.

The story, told in the first person, described the mood of a boy walking along the ocean shore one morning after the death or the funeral—in any case, after the loss, of a schoolmate or neighbor, or perhaps a relative. It was remarkable that in spite of much vagueness in the incidents, the sense of loss, a kind of diffused sadness, made the story poignant from the very beginning. I suppose the description of shore and surf and horizon evoked this mood.

Suddenly another figure appeared, coming down the beach, a boy of about the same age as the imagined narrator of the incident. The two met as though they were keeping a *rendez-vous*. Their greetings were casual, natural, and subtly affectionate. None of us listening to the story for the first time failed to grasp the weird drama of the quietly told incident. The boy who came walking along the beach was the friend who had caused the mood of sadness, the friend who had been drowned.

That was the whole story. Why the lifelike ghost returned, when, or in what circumstances the drowning had occurred, in what manner the apparition vanished again, the story did not say, nor did we care. The incident was told with amazing power. It convinced us, yet not as actual experience convinces. For some reason on which I could not put my finger, I asked Talbot whether he had thought of the story while he was awake, or whether he had dreamed it. It was a dream, he said. So far as I now recall, I made no further comment, nor did any of the class. Yet it was a rare feat to suggest in words the dream mood, the other-worldly nostalgia, or regret, or yearning. I ought to have urged Talbot at once to seize all such fragile material whenever it came within reach, and to put into a story every one of the sensitive perceptions which belong to his temperament. I was so amazed by the story that I am not sure now whether I told him how much I admired it.

While I taught composition at Amherst I had at least this excuse for failing to encourage the individuality of each young writer; in my own writing I had not yet found myself. But in the literature classes I did somewhat better. After a year or two I developed a simple theory for teaching the love of books, a theory which I stated in an essay which *The Nation* published on September 3, 1908,[3] I still hold these convictions, with little or no change.

In the enjoyment of life itself our students are not a whit behind the youth of fifty years ago. Perhaps it is their curiosity to get at life, to have experience, that makes them at times seem impatient with books. Of their own choice they read stories, no matter how crude, that present life with zest and energy. Should not the first principle of teaching literature be to discover what prevents life-loving youth from seeing the life stored up in other books, as yet dead to him? Should not the second principle be to remove that obstacle, whatever it is? If there is a third principle, should it not be to see that the student reads as many books as possible? To be at home in any art we must constantly hear or see examples of it. . . .

If this statement of the general problem is just, a college course in literature should provide for two things—the direct contact of the student's mind with as many books as possible, and the filling in of any gaps in his sympathy with what he reads. Almost all the great books were intended for the average man, and the author contemplated an immediate relation with his audience. There is room for the annotator or teacher only when time has made the subject remote or strange, or when the reader's imagination is unable to grasp the recorded experience. A book fails to interest young people because it is of another age, or because they are imaginatively immature. The business of the teacher, then, is to supply the historical or imaginative approach. Otherwise the book should speak for itself. . . .

A glance at most college catalogs will show that very different theories of teaching literature are not uncommon.

[3] *The Memory*, p. 183.

Courses on the development of this form, or the structure of that, or the romantic something else! Valuable though such studies may prove to the well-read scholar, they are useless to the unread. By their very nature they thrust a screen of historical and critical apparatus between pupil and book, and the reading itself, what there is of it, tends to become a search for literary data to sustain the theory, rather than a vital experience. . . .

If the pupil's task is to read great books constantly, the teacher's part, to connect the reading with the pupil's experience, is large and difficult. When we consider the wide knowledge he must have of boys and of books, we need not be surprised if the successful teacher is rare. He must recover for the student those past ideas from which the book grew, and to which it appealed. At the same time he must use his tact to keep in the foreground the book itself, rather than its history. . . .

How about the teacher's own love of books? The fact seems to be that only a few teachers of literature are habitual, enthusiastic readers of the books they blame their students for not reading. Their chosen companions are not Spenser, Shakespeare, Milton, Dickens, Thackeray. Of course they know the books. They may still remember what a book is about, but if they have forgotten what pleasure it gave them, how can they communicate the lost zest? Too often we hear a teacher confess comfortably, over his cigar or his pipe, "Somehow Dickens doesn't take hold of me as he used to," in a tone that makes it look dark for Dickens. If our delight in Mrs. Gamp or Mr. Pecksniff is undimmed and we begin to defend our taste, we probably find that the professor has not read Dickens recently. He will lecture on him, however, at a moment's notice.

The pity of it is that to interest a boy in a book nothing

may be needed but a sincere word of intimate praise. In school during study hour Jim detects Bill with a non-academic volume under the desk, and starts inquiries, to which Bill responds from the nearest side of his mouth, "It's *Huckleberry Finn*. Gee, it's great!" And Jim is filled with the desire to read. But imagine the result if Jim's father had said at the dinner table, "James, I wish you to read *Huckleberry Finn*. Every boy should read it. Some critics think Mark Twain our greatest novelist. The story is of the picaresque type," etc.

Finally, the teacher of literature should if possible be a writer. The creative habit of mind, no matter how modestly exercised, is the surest of all protections against pedantry.

2

English composition, and English literature. There was a third subject, not mentioned when President Harris invited me to teach at Amherst, but often stressed there by visiting preachers and by successful graduates returning to impart to teachers and students alike the secret of success. I soon learned from the puzzling re-iteration that whatever else the College gave her sons, the most precious gift was training in character.

This would have been good news if I could have believed that Amherst or any other American college had the right to claim that it specialized or excelled in the training of character. Though I had been teaching for only a short time, I already began to doubt that a college course would necessarily make a student more industrious, more dependable, more honorable, more sensitive to unselfish ideals.

It was not my intention then, and it is not now, to indict the colleges exclusively. The parents who send their children to an institution of higher learning, rarely mention character as one of the things to be learned. Their hope is that their offspring will come out not much weaker morally than they went in. So long as the family, who must bear the loss, are not worried about the absence of character training, don't imagine that the colleges will do much worrying. Where morality—personal obligation and responsibility —is not taught from the cradle up, an educational system may become a costly folly.

Before I attempt to make good this charge, let me notice two exceptions. Military schools, particularly the academies at West Point and Annapolis, teach responsibility and train character. Though preparation for war should not be the chief business of civilized society, the soldier-making institutions are still the only schools which within their field develop measurably, moral strength as well as physical and mental. Apparently the schools which prepare for peace do not believe that the peaceful need courage, or endurance, or the spirit of devotion. That is, with the other exception, the Roman Catholic schools. They too inculcate a system of personal ethics, and develop character.

In school and college we have long neglected the training of the mind, but we excused ourselves by saying with the returning graduate that we excelled in character building. Yet perhaps we have little right to claim more success in character building than in mental training. The student can pass the course by mastering part of it. An incomplete knowledge of enough courses leads to a degree. To describe the result of this undigested nibbling we misuse the noble word "culture." This kind of culture is supposed to spring from intellectual indolence surrounded by architecture, preferably Gothic. But education is, among other things, a business. What little the students learn could be acquired in a short time, but we'd rather keep that secret to ourselves for the sake of tuition fees. We spread the notion that the slower you are in getting your culture, the thicker it is and the longer it sticks. Is this education, or is it a racket?

Whatever it is, we have had the grace to drop from it the teaching of morality or ethics. There are courses in ethics, but we make the subject elective, as though gravitation were optional. There are still chapel services, but they are unpopular, especially with the faculty; if they survive, it is because they serve to get the students out of bed all at the same time, or approximately so. No device has been hit on for putting them to bed again at the end of the day, but it is hoped the fixed rising bell will automatically, after fifteen or more hours, bring on a uniform weariness.

Chapel services were instituted when the spiritual life of the student was thought important, and they are declining now that outward well-being comes first and inner states are ignored. Yet teachers know that the life of what used to be called the soul is still present; that youth still is aware of a difference between the temporary and the timeless, and still more, of the difference between right and wrong; that in varying degrees the young have a sense of duty, an obligation to something higher and more lasting than themselves; that for this reaching toward eternal ideals they crave expression.

If this craving is thwarted, they usually go one of two ways. They stop thinking of remote goals and permanent satisfactions. They settle down to the career of a trained animal. They are content with the hour, even cheerful. They are well-mannered, quiet, affectionate. But they will not change the world, nor solve its problems.

Or if the craving of youth for ideal things cannot be stamped out but must survive, pent-up and suffocating, sooner or later the victim takes his trouble to a psychologist, a tactful person who talks about the "psyche" and never mentions the soul. What to religion was a problem for his personal will, to be solved by his personal decision, to psychology is an affliction or a disease, the cure of which rests with somebody else. No longer a moral being, he becomes a "case."

As the colleges and schools ceased to draw on religion for character building, they put faith rather vaguely in sports. Perhaps the training table would teach self-denial, the teamwork would teach cooperation, close competition or violent conflict would teach daring and endurance, excellent virtues all, and not one of them otherwise included in the curriculum. Furthermore, sports were to provide an education for the student who merely cheered from the bleachers—they would exercise his instincts of loyalty.

I should be the last to scoff at idealization of one's school. Loyalty has no doubt proved the driving force in many a noble career. The spell that the fruitful colleges have laid upon the more sensitive of their children may be a precious kind of education, but I doubt if athletics ever had much to do with it. Anything wholesome, that is. Athletics is a business, conducted by the college authorities, who in business are not amateurs, though they want the players to seem so. Victory in the games is more desired than progress in the classroom. No professor is thought so necessary as the coach, and none is paid so much. The players may not be subsidized, but they often are, in one way or another, and their fellow students, understanding the situation, are not offended at it, unless the large-hearted alumnus who puts a camouflaged professional through college, for the greater glory of Alma Mater, happens to pick a second- or third-rate professional.

No boy is happily prepared for life by watching such a system at close range, knowing that his college lends herself willingly to a perversion which yields advertising and cash.

In the spring of my second year at Amherst the Columbia baseball team came up to play on Pratt Field, and played very well indeed. The Amherst boys helped themselves to some solace in defeat by hinting that one of the successful adversaries was a minor league player, well known throughout New England. When I asked Mr. Nelligan, the Amherst coach, if this was true, he smiled philosophically and urged me not to be disturbed, since it might happen anywhere.

I wrote to the chairman of the Columbia Alumni Committee which then had charge of sports; I told him what was said about us in Amherst, and asked what reasons he had for thinking the charge unjust. He answered with a show of moral indignation that he could find in my letter nothing to substantiate the charges I made, and he thought Columbia had a right to expect from one of her graduates a more loyal spirit. I replied with some heat that he missed the point. I didn't want to prove the player a ringer; on the contrary, I was asking for evidence, for something in his Columbia record, with which to silence the Amherst charges. The player, I need hardly add, finished out the spring schedule, and then disappeared from the Columbia campus, having rendered the service for which he had been imported. The chairman of the Committee on Athletics did not disappear. When I went back to Columbia to teach, he was one of the University Trustees, very friendly to me, always. When I was elected to the Vestry of Old Trinity, I found him already a member of the Board. I have heard him lament the decay of true piety and the lack of character in the young.

In the autumn following the Columbia team incident, an unusually promising student entered Amherst with the freshman class. He had good looks, good manners, good habits, a better outfit of brains than freshmen sometimes bring with them. He impressed all his teachers by the thoroughness, the neatness and the dispatch with which he did his work. If he looked older than he said he was, we explained the illusion by his intellectual and moral maturity. In the spring he came out for baseball, and what talent he had for the sport! It shocked us to learn from rival college teams, defeated and angry, that he was a professional, playing with us under an assumed name. The indignant college authorities expelled him promptly, I suppose for the fib or perjury rather than for the intended infraction of the amateur rule.

The alumnus who had backed him, shared the opinion of the college disciplinarians. "Why didn't the boy have more character? I sent him to school and gave him the opportunity to get a fine education. If he had played on the team, openly, how could anyone object? Many a boy on the glee club earns money by singing in a church choir."

I cite these two incidents from my early years as a teacher, not to approve or condemn the rules which were then in force to control college athletics, and certainly not to imply that college athletes in general were professionals in disguise. I am sure the majority of the boys on the Columbia and Amherst baseball teams had a clear record, and I have first-hand knowledge of their excellence as students. But it was not helpful to the moral sensitiveness of the student body as a whole to know that occasional crookedness occurred, and that it was expected to occur.

In those early years of my teaching I was learning, perhaps, more than I taught; among other things I was learning in the ironies of college life something about the ironies which must be reckoned with in all human society. The art of writing and the love of good literature cannot be taught in a vacuum. The total behavior of all the students, of all the teachers, and of the other college authorities, will always modify—strengthen or weaken—the best that the classroom can impart. It is just as well, but perhaps the university which grants the prospective teacher his doctorate should warn him in plain terms that to some extent a teacher of literature, or anything else, must find his own inner defense against cynicism. The official pretensions of a college to train character may be taken seriously as an ideal, but not as a fact.

CHAPTER IV

Teacher in a Country College

1

IN 1903 when I went to Amherst, the great western State universities were beginning to threaten the prestige of the East, and the eastern universities were acquiring an influence which disturbed the graduates of small colleges like Amherst and Williams. On every campus there was much talk of the advantages and disadvantages of the smaller institutions as contrasted with the large. These discussions were fruitful only as expressions of individual pieties and loyalties. Few graduates had attended both a small college and a large university. The plea for one type of institution or the other was usually supported by neither experience nor facts.

It was said that in a small college the student would receive his instruction in small groups and would therefore come into closer contact with the professors. Even if the facts here had been as stated, the question would have remained whether the teachers in the small college were as worth knowing intimately as the teachers in the large. It seemed to be a growing fashion for the most promising of younger teachers to accept calls to the larger places.

And it wasn't true that in the smaller colleges the classes were smaller. Only the universities in those days could afford a faculty large enough to hold down the size of classes. In my first years at

Amherst I was charged with the instruction of all the freshmen, numbering about one hundred and twenty. President Harris rather thought I could handle them in two sections of sixty each. After one week's experiment I divided them into four sections of thirty each, doubling the amount of my teaching hours in order to give my pupils at least the attention I myself had received at Columbia. The four sections of my three-hour-a-week course took up twelve hours, and in addition I read one hundred and twenty themes a week, and consulted each student on his work. No other teacher of English at Amherst had ever, so far as I could learn, taken his duties so seriously. Neither the President nor any of my colleagues said a word to suggest that so much work was expected of me.

I soon began to feel that the contrast should be not between a small college and a large university, but between an institution in the country and one in a city. The education which any school offers is qualified—that is, enriched or limited—by the community in which the instruction is imparted. In Amherst the students were educated by the township and the townsfolk almost as much as by classroom instruction. At Columbia the students had a large part of their education from New York. Illustrations of this contrast are so obvious we hardly need mention them. At Amherst the new economic and social problems of our time had been heard of. Professor James Crook, who taught economics, was successful, I think, in awakening his brightest pupils to what were shortly to become lively issues in American life. To show his boys what he was talking of, he arranged trips to Boston or New York City, and investigated actual conditions among working people. In Amherst there was a small hat-factory, but in no sense was the little village an industrial center.

While I was at Amherst there was no form of theatrical amusement, no theatre, and as yet no motion picture house. Occasionally a play came to Northampton, more often to Springfield, but the student of the drama had to visit Boston or New York to see the progress or the decline of his subject.

Another contrast between the city university and the country college I felt keenly. Amherst offered only the so-called cultural courses usual in colleges. There was no law school, no medical school, no engineering school. At Columbia the college undergraduate associated constantly in his fraternity house and in the other campus meeting places with students more mature than himself whose heads were full of ideas which, if he hadn't talked with them, he would probably not have met at that period in his life.

So much for the student. The difference between the country college and the city university could be traced also in the faculty. With only a limited number of cultural subjects to teach, there could be no great intellectual stir on the college campus. During my Amherst years research or productive scholarship of any kind was not particularly noticeable among my colleagues. Their companionship was delightful but not intellectually stimulating. Professor Genung was an exception. He was busy with his works of biblical criticism, and he was an indefatigable reader, but his productive life was drawing to a close. He had made his mark with his famous textbooks on rhetoric. During my six years at Amherst, as I remember, he got out one volume—on the ancient Hebrew literature. I was the only other person in the department who published anything.

Will Nitze, coming like me from the university background, and with the intellectual momentum of the university still in him, pushed ahead in his researches into Medieval French literature and published the results. No one else in the language groups so far as I know published a word, though these teachers were scholarly men, particularly Harry deForest Smith, Professor of Greek, whose great erudition was modern and inspiring, if only he had had the disposition to give it to the world.

The country colleges must have been in a state of transition just then. A few years later it began to look as though they were in a state of dry rot. The unproductive attitude of some teachers, my seniors, seems in retrospect unbelievable. The colleagues who were one grade above me—on the average ten years older than I—led a pleasant but lazy life. They thought they worked hard and they believed, no doubt sincerely, that evenings spent playing bridge and excursions to neighboring taverns for jolly dinner parties, were essential recreation or refreshment. The elder generation of Amherst teachers, the famous elders, some of whom still survived on the campus, had won reputation for their college, and international fame for themselves, by no such indolent philosophy.

One Saturday evening a colleague dropped in to smoke a pipe or two by my fireside, and finding me at my books and my writing, he gave me a first-rate dressing down, all with the friendliest intentions. He feared I was too ambitious; overwork never did anyone any good; I would enjoy a better reputation with him and his generation on the faculty if I relaxed more often, gave evidence of more human tendencies, even human weaknesses. In plain words, this kindly man—no scholar certainly but in many respects a good teacher, and according to his lights a devoted one—hinted that God would be glad to forgive me if on occasion I should get drunk, or should develop more interest in the other sex than my neighbors had yet been able to detect in me.

I report an actual conversation, but lest I misrepresent my colleagues, I had better sketch the portrait of the Amherst faculty as they were when I joined them in 1903.

2

They fell into three distinct groups. There were first of all, the great veterans, well-established in the world of scholarship, and relaxing, if at all, only because their energies flagged as they approached the age of retirement.

Easily first in this group, the Amherst alumni would have placed the Professor of Philosophy, Charles Edward Garman. In 1903 he still taught his classes, but his health was failing, and in his invalid condition he withdrew from society except as he met his students in the classroom or in private talks at his home. I saw him only at faculty meetings, which he attended regularly but where he never spoke. I cannot now recall the sound of his voice, but I see clearly his fine head and his dark piercing eyes, which had a kind of hypnotic influence upon all who came in his presence. I am not sure what his private philosophy was, but he certainly was a marvelous psychologist quite in the modern sense, no matter how old-fashioned his philosophy may have seemed. He could teach boys to think if the capacity for thought was in them. As a teacher, and perhaps as a thinker, he was past his prime, but his influence with graduates, with undergraduates, with the town of Amherst, indeed with the whole countryside, was prodigious. Professor F. J. E. Woodbridge, of Columbia, and Professor James Hayden Tufts, of Chicago University, were only the best known of his many pupils.

A more vigorous personality, though the Garman admirers might not have agreed with me that he was a far greater man, was Benjamin Kendall Emerson, Professor of Geology. He seemed to belong among the Amherst patriarchs, his white beard supplying the effect of many years.

Like most of the Amherst old guard, he had had his training among the famous scholars of Europe, and he belonged to the day when the American small college was not small in its outlook, but resembled the small universities of Germany, where research prospered sometimes more happily than in the hubbub and distractions of Berlin.

He had studied at Göttingen and Berlin, and had served as assistant on the German Geological Survey. He also pursued his private researches in Switzerland, Saxony, Bohemia, and Norway. In 1890 he was appointed Assistant Geologist to the United States Geological Survey. In 1896 he was appointed Geologist. In 1897 he was a Vice-President of the International Geological Congress at St. Petersburg. He visited Siberia, and with Fridtjof Nansen traveled through Norway. He was President of the Geological Society of America and a Fellow of the American Academy of Arts and Sciences.

As I knew him in Amherst he was a great teacher, working quietly in his laboratory and gathering the valuable mineral collection which is one of the College's treasures. Self-reliant and independent in all his ways, he developed many picturesque traits, and gave rise to innumerable legends. An Amherst senior called on him one day to ask for a recommendation. "Professor Emerson, I am applying for the post of mathematics teacher in such-and-such a school."

"Are you?" said Emerson, with courteous interest.

"I haven't been in your classes, Professor Emerson—"

"That is true."

"—and you don't know me very well—"

"As a matter of fact, I don't know you at all."

"Yes, Professor, but since I am an Amherst student and one of the graduating class, I hoped that perhaps you could give me some kind of testimonial. Your name would carry enormous weight."

Emerson reached for his pen. "I'll give you a testimonial with pleasure."

"Thanks ever so much, Professor."

Emerson wrote a few lines, put the paper in an envelope, gave it to the boy with a bow, saying he was always glad to be of service. On the sidewalk the boy opened the envelope and read:

"To Whom It May Concern: Mr. Blank, who says he is a member of the senior class in Amherst College, desires me to certify to his eligibility as a teacher of mathematics.

"Of his mathematical talents and training, I can say nothing, never having laid eyes on him until five minutes ago.

"Of his character the reader must judge, since, knowing that I am totally unacquainted with him, he has been willing to accept a recommendation from me."

Stories of Emerson's absent-mindedness were countless. More than once during my Amherst years he drove his horse and buggy into the hills on a week-end search for minerals. Having hitched the horse to a tree, he would climb up an interesting rock surface, and more likely than not would come down on the other side the mountain, where the sight of a trolley track would suggest an easy way to get home. Late that night he might wake up and wonder what had happened to the horse.

The story which I like best tells of a shopping expedition one afternoon to Springfield. In a haberdasher's where he had been buying neckties and such gear most of his life, he made several purchases and told the clerk to charge them. The young man, a new arrival in Springfield, naturally asked Emerson his name. Emerson couldn't remember. He went through his pockets but there were no letters. By bad luck he happened not to be wearing his Phi Beta Kappa key. On his watch were initials, but they recalled nothing to him.

"Never mind," said the clerk. "Take the goods along and pay for them the next time you come this way."

Emerson, unwilling to do business in such a haphazard way, declined the offer and was leaving the shop when an Amherst student came in.

"Good afternoon, Professor Emerson."

"That's the name!"

Though we thought of Professor Emerson as one of the original giants who had set Amherst College in its fine tradition, we had daily sight of a still older generation, retired from active service yet continuing to exercise strong influence. Chief among these were William Cole Esty, Emeritus Professor of Mathematics, and Edward Hitchcock, "Old Doc," former Professor of Anatomy and of Hygiene, the health officer of the College, and in spite of service far past the age of retirement, its titular Dean.

Of these two men, in spite of Old Doc's extraordinary popularity, Professor Esty was, I believe, more significant in the whole faculty picture. He was born in 1838. After the death of his wife, Martha Anne Cushing, in 1887, he lived with his sister-in-law, Mrs. Edward Tuckerman, Sara Elizabeth Sigurney Cushing. Professor Tuckerman had died in 1886. The Tuckerman home, one of the most remarkable in America, was located at the southern end of the village, near the Boston and Maine station, on the edge of what would have been the Common if the town had extended the Common so far.

In my day we spoke of the Tuckerman house, or the Esty house, without much regard to its history or to the original ownership. It was a long stone building of the English manor type, facing westward toward South Pleasant Street. On the left, or northern side, was a spacious library filled with remarkable books, many of them on scientific subjects, but many of them also dealing with history and literature. Here and there through the room reading desks were placed for convenience in consulting heavy volumes. At the western end was a large fireplace. On the northern side an immense bay window provided excellent light for daytime study, and an intimate view of the garden.

West of the library the house extended itself, as it seemed, indefinitely. The dining room was a banquet hall. The living quarters upstairs had once housed Professor Esty's children and later his grandchildren. When he and Mrs. Edward Tuckerman, in their declining years, moved to a more modest home in Worcester, easier to care for in the social changes which came with the First World War, the Tuckerman house was acquired by an Amherst fraternity. It certainly was large enough. It might have been turned into a hotel.

Professor Esty and Mrs. Tuckerman were delightful and hospitable friends, and when I consider the reasons why the American country college was once of vital importance in our educational history, I recall the Tuckerman home, and what the house itself and the dwellers in it stood for.

Professor Esty in his years of active teaching may or may not have been an original or pathbreaking mathematician. He represents to me a type of all-round culture, urbane and cosmopolitan, which today we should look for in vain at small colleges, perhaps even at most universities. Like Professor Emerson and like Edward Tuckerman he had been inspired in youth by German scholarship in the romantic period. The graduate work which had prepared him for his career was quite different from the amassing of academic credits which today earns an American Ph.D. In the noble days of Göttingen and Leipzig, two universities which particularly attracted American students, the love of truth was kindled, and the passion for disinterested research. Apparently it made little difference to young men who brought home from Europe this dynamic equipment whether they taught in small places or large. In either they could pursue their studies and share their knowledge with any eager inquirers who sought them out. They had a tendency, like the great scholars who taught them, to become somewhat solitary and retired, their intellectual curiosity never flagged, their philosophy did not permit them to become indolent, their way of life satisfied a spiritual need, and they all enjoyed, or so it seemed, peace of mind and profound satisfaction. Among their neighbors at Amherst they were held in awe and veneration, as models of character and lofty ambition.

On the occasions when I dined at the Tuckerman house the fine talk was led by the Professor and Mrs. Tuckerman, with the witty collaboration of Tom Esty and his wife, that rare soul, Annette Emerson. Professor Esty, Senior, talked much about English literature, I suppose in deference to my interests. One winter, as I recall, he was preoccupied with Sir Walter Scott, spending practically all his time re-reading the Waverley novels. Loss of memory he described as a benign provision of Nature. Never could he have found new novels to compare with Scott's, but since he had forgotten them entirely, they now burst upon him with a triple surprise. The plot and the characters were fresh; since once he had known them, they brought back a peculiar aroma of youth, and since he had learned something by much living, he now discovered unsuspected values in the characters and the plots.

Perhaps the unique charm of his personality was not, after all, so unique; perhaps he symbolized and continued for me and for others at Amherst the qualities of Edward Tuckerman, his brother-in-law, whose good taste and wealth had built the house twenty years or more before I was born, and who died when I was six years old. If I were writing the history of the ideals and practice of scholarship which once made Amherst an educational center, I should begin with Edward Tuckerman. Though I never laid eyes on him, his character and his spirit, as passed on to the Amherst of my day, still seem very much alive.

He was born in Boston in 1817, the son of a prosperous merchant. After graduation from Harvard Law School in 1839, he spent several years in Europe studying philosophy, history, and botany. In particular, he studied at Upsala, Sweden, under Elias Fries, the famous lichenologist. His studies with Fries eventually determined his career and led to his fame as the first authority on North American lichens. His scholarly curiosity was encyclopedic. When he came to Amherst in the late 1850's, it was to teach history. In 1858 he was appointed Professor of Botany. He had already published monographs on American lichens, and was earning the reputation which associates him with his friend Asa Gray. Toward the end of his life he lost his hearing, but he continued his researches with undiminished vigor, and wrote much on subjects not connected with lichenology. He had a passion for antiquarian and genealogical research, for philosophy, for divinity, and for law. According to the Amherst legend, he had extraordinary social gifts, and in that library of his where I enjoyed in my day delightful hours, he had entertained, with all the graces as well as the solidities of scholarship, some of his most distinguished contemporaries, American or European.

Perhaps it was easier for me to imagine his personality and cherish his memory because his nephew, Frederick Tuckerman, (1857-1929) was a neighbor and friend of mine, Junior Warden at Grace Church, the little Episcopal parish where during my Amherst years I played the organ and served on the Vestry.

Dr. Frederick Tuckerman, after taking his degree at the Harvard Medical School in 1882, studied in London, Berlin, and Heidelberg.

Except for a short period when he lectured on anatomy and physiology at the Massachusetts Agricultural College, he lived quietly in Amherst, pursuing his researches on the gustatory and.taste organs, engaging in local town affairs and producing at intervals, in the cultured leisure which private means permitted, works dealing with comparative anatomy and natural history, and with New England genealogy.

Every Monday afternoon Dr. Tuckerman, knowing that I would be at my desk in the study on the second floor of Mrs. Marsh's house, would stop in for a few minutes to talk about the music at the church services the day before, or to discuss a new book he was reading, or to recall some memory of Alfred Tennyson which he had from his father, who had known the English laureate. In his student days abroad Dr. Fred had visited all the shrines, literary or historical, and even as late as 1903 he lived as much as possible in an English or Victorian atmosphere, and modeled his life, like his uncle before him, on English taste and character. He seemed always to have more leisure than the rest of us, yet he was an industrious man, as we can see from the record of his accomplishments in the *Dictionary of American Biography*.

If the Tuckermans, Edward and Frederick, enriched Amherst with an English tradition, most of the others in the elder generation of scholars imported the habits and customs they had learned at Heidelberg, Göttingen, and Leipzig. Professor Elijah Paddock Harris, for example, vigorous and original teacher of chemistry, made of his German memories almost a religion. Born in 1832, he had grown up an American country boy, but in his youth at the University of Göttingen he had watched world-famous scientists at work, and he refused to admit other ideals of study or teaching than theirs. I don't know who among his teachers passed on to him his rather ferocious notion of pedagogy. He expected the youngest student to illustrate from his first day in the laboratory the spirit of scientific research, and to burn always with the pure flame of truth. Since the Amherst undergraduate at times fell short of this ideal, the impassioned professor used more than one class hour to pour maledictions on the lazy and the stupid.

After an examination one week he posted the entire class as failing. At the next recitation he did not appear, and a bewildered student asked when they were to meet again. Old Harris snapped at him, "Meet you in hell!" This outburst provoked a complaint that the Professor might be a good chemist, but his manners were crude. The criticism struck home. The Professor agreed to meet his charges once more, if only to explain why they all deserved a zero. They gathered in the laboratory. On the long desk from behind which he imparted the science of chemistry, rested a vile-looking, vile-smelling, black pot.

"There's not a chemist in the class!" he roared. "You're all too delicate. When I studied under the great scientists of Germany, I learned to stop at nothing, no matter how unpleasant. A chemist must have courage and backbone. Also he must have eyesight. There isn't one good eye among you!"

He picked up the black pot and sniffed at it. "Suppose you had to find out what is in this?"

He stuck his finger into the revolting mess, tasted it, smacked his lips, then with a wicked grin passed the pot along the row of students, challenging them to imitate his heroic curiosity. They accepted the invitation, not daring to decline. One by one they turned green and made a dash for the washroom. The Professor waited patiently till they were able to return.

"Now, boys, if you had half the eyesight of a chemist, you would have noticed that I stuck my first finger into the pot, but sucked my little finger."

I first met the fierce old man at a faculty reception. He greeted me cordially, in his own way. "I wish you luck in your teaching, but you probably won't have any. You will tell your students to study certain pages, and when you meet them you'll ask questions to see whether they obeyed you. If they really have, you'll congratulate them and give them a good mark. Bosh!"

"What else should I do, Professor Harris?"

He glared at me. "When I tell my students to study pages fifty to one hundred, I begin my questions at page one hundred, not page fifty. I want to know whether a boy is serious, and whether he has an ounce of curiosity in him. Did he read only what he had to, or did he push on?"

When the ladies of the College asked me to give some talks on the English poets,[1] Mrs. Elijah Harris thanked me with considerable emotion for my remarks on Byron. "I have a special fondness for that poet, Mr. Erskine. When the Professor studied in Germany long ago, he was courting me by mail, and all his letters contained pages and pages of Byron."

Edward Payson Crowell, for many years Amherst's remarkable teacher of Latin, was two years older than Elijah Harris, but at the close of his career when I knew him he was afflicted with total blindness, and it was somewhat hard for a newcomer to realize that he had once been one of the most active professors and citizens in the town. In 1903 he was seventy-three years old, but though sightless he still conducted recitations with advanced pupils, and his remarkable memory made his instruction as effective, or so I was told, as though the text had been open before him.

In 1879, the year of my birth, he served as member of the Massachusetts House of Representatives, and to the end of his life his interest in public affairs was lively and well informed. His equipment in modern as well as ancient languages was unusual. His first Amherst appointment had been to teach German and Greek. Latin became his specialty later. He was quite at home, of course, in Italian, French, and Spanish. I once heard him ask Will Nitze what proportion of Latin derivatives were already firmly planted in the English language at the time of the Norman conquest.

In Professor Crowell's youth his running mate, as it were, in the teaching of the classics, was Professor William Seymour Tyler, (1810-1897). Professor Tyler was for over half a century a quite

[1] *The Memory*, p. 162.

fabulous teacher of the Greek language and Greek culture to every boy who earned the Amherst degree. Like Professor Crowell he was also a fine public citizen, serving the town whenever called upon and accepting any administrative duty the College put upon him. Like Professor Edward Tuckermans', his influence lingered in a startling kind of immortality.

William Seymour Tyler had several sons, all of whom became teachers. John Mason Tyler (1851-1929) was the Professor of Biology at Amherst, as gracious and well-loved a personality as I ever knew. He adored the memory of his great father, and perhaps his pious affection made us all feel more strongly the continuing presence of the masterful Greek teacher. Dean Woodbridge at Columbia never tired of describing the methods and the extraordinary vigor with which old Professor Tyler had made Homer and Plato and Sophocles come alive for him.

John Tyler had learned his science at Göttingen and Leipzig. John Franklin Genung (1850-1919), teacher of rhetoric and composition, had studied Hebrew at the University of Leipzig. In my Amherst days he was teaching biblical literature and English literature, and in his scholarly life he was illustrating the careful and tireless methods which he had learned at the German university. The study in his home was large and full of books, and expressive of Genung's peculiarities and whimsies. He always wrote with a quill pen. A bundle of quills lay on his desk, and every morning he sharpened a fresh pen for the day's work. A special apparatus over a large inkwell held the pens so that the points, constantly immersed, were prevented from drying and shriveling.

In his beautiful manuscripts he always illuminated the initial letter of each chapter. When a new book went to the publisher, the lettering of the text was exactly the size of the type he wished. Footnotes were written in smaller letters, which indicated again the precise size of the desired type.

Like all these elder scholars of the old Amherst faculty, he had prodigious powers of concentration. Once started on a piece of work, he would keep at it until it was finished. Often, he told me he had been writing all night, and I recall one incident which he did not seem to think extraordinary; he mentioned it after his return from a vacation trip to England. He had gone over for a rest and for long walks in the English countryside, but on arriving he stopped for a night in London, and at dinner he had an attractive idea for a paper. Before retiring for the night he began the essay, and it went so well that he wrote till dawn. After a morning nap he felt like writing some more. He managed to finish the essay the day before his boat sailed for America. That evening he walked around London in the long twilight, and next morning he started for Southampton, entirely happy, with his new manuscript in his bag.

3

The second group of the Amherst faculty after the famous elders were represented for me by George Daniel Olds, William Lyman Cowles, and Arthur Lalanne Kimball. I name these three not only because they were close and inseparable friends, but because their excellent scholarship had an American as well as a European background. Professor Olds, who taught mathematics, had studied in Heidelberg and Berlin. He came to Amherst from a professorship in the University of Rochester, where he had been an undergraduate. Succeeding Dr. Hitchcock as the Amherst Dean, he was elected President of the College to succeed Dr. Meikeljohn. Professor Cowles, who taught Latin, was a constant visitor in Italy, often taking with him well-prepared students to do research in Roman antiquities. He had studied, after graduation from Amherst, at the University of Berlin. Professor Kimball, physicist, graduate of Princeton, pursued his advanced studies at Johns Hopkins and came to Amherst from a professorship at that university.

These three were a link between the great Amherst teachers of the past and the youngest members of the faculty. They were remarkable in their own right, but they revered their predecessors.

Along with these three my memory associates Arthur John Hopkins, who during my first six years at Amherst assisted the picturesque Elijah Paddock Harris, and later succeeded him. Professor Hopkins was a tall gentleman, inclined to be thin, of a thoughtful disposition, well endowed with humor. Impressed by his long legs, the students called him "Hoppie." He lived on the west side of South Pleasant Street, just under the old South Dormitory. In 1903 his family consisted of his gifted wife, Margaret Sutton Briscoe, the short story writer; his small daughter, Cornelia, now Mrs. David Allen, and his mother-in-law, Mrs. Briscoe, whimsical and entertaining Baltimorean, with the warmest of hearts. On Sunday evenings Professor and Mrs. Hopkins kept open house to students, especially to those who had the ambition or perhaps the ability to write. Mrs. Hopkins was in literary matters a natural educator, and the students doubtless learned much from her talk about her profession. I certainly found it profitable to miss nothing she said.

One evening she called my attention to a poet already well known in England, but not yet firmly established in the United States. It was the first time I heard his name, though his marvelous little book, *A Shropshire Lad,* first appeared in England in 1896. The ghost of A. E. Housman would be astonished to know how intimately it is associated with a pleasant parlor in a New England college town.

Mrs. Briscoe's kind and impulsive nature entertained us from year-end to year-end. The Rector of the Episcopal church had a sorrowful way of reading the Scriptures, as though he were recounting against his will a ghastly tragedy. There was a legend in Amherst that the first time Mrs. Briscoe heard the mournful cadences she stopped after the service with her own peculiar consolation.

"Rector, it was all so long ago and so far away, and historians make so many errors, perhaps it never happened at all."

During my earlier Amherst residence she prepared one day to attend a faculty tea. To reach the party she climbed the hill on which the old dormitories stand, and started to walk past them. It was January, and ice covered the path. Mrs. Briscoe's feet slipped from under her and she came down flat on her back. I heard her tell the incident.

"I had on my best white gloves. How could I put a hand to the ground? I just cast an eye on all the dormitory windows to be sure none of those horrid boys were laughing at me. Then I relaxed comfortably where I was and took off my gloves slowly, finger by finger. When the gloves were safe I scrambled up, went on to the tea, and really made a sensation. Everybody wanted to know how I got the mud between my shoulders, but I wouldn't tell them!"

Professor Hopkins, himself an Amherst graduate, was a well-trained scientist and an excellent teacher. His hobby was the history of alchemy, about which he was writing a book when I last saw him.

4

The third group of the Amherst faculty was made up of newcomers like Will Nitze and myself. When Nitze resigned to accept a professorship in California, he was succeeded by Henry Carrington Lancaster, who in 1919 became Professor of French Literature and Chairman of the department of Romance Languages at Johns Hopkins. Lancaster's friend, Lewis Chamberlayne, came to Amherst to assist Professor Cowles in the teaching of Latin, but before long resigned to accept a professorship at the University of South Carolina. Ernest Wilkins, my old comrade in the Baxter Marsh house, left Amherst to teach Italian at the University of Chicago, and from that post went to be President of Oberlin University. Newcomers in the sciences, in history, or in various literatures, came and went with the same disconcerting speed. I returned to Columbia in 1909.

Here was a puzzle for an educational theorist to solve. President Harris, kind gentleman, growing a little weary of his task, honored the eldest generation of Amherst scholars as much as any one. He knew also that the old dynamic teaching and productive scholarship was disappearing from that second or middle group of his teachers. He succeeded in attracting a group of youngsters who were ambitious and on the whole far above the average in teaching and in scholarly research. But he could not keep them. For a reason which he found too baffling, they all moved on.

CHAPTER V

President Meiklejohn

1

IN 1912 Dr. George Harris resigned the presidency of Amherst College, and the Trustees elected as his successor Dr. Alexander Meiklejohn, Professor of Logic and Metaphysics and Dean at Brown University. The new administration started off briskly, but progress was interrupted or postponed by the First World War. When the college resumed its peacetime functions in the winter of 1918-1919, a serious strain was apparent between the President and his faculty, and to an increasing degree between him and his Trustees. At the Commencement of 1923 his resignation was announced.

Mr. Meiklejohn was a gifted teacher, a magnetic leader of youth. So far as I know he made no pretentions to special scholarship, but he sharpened the wits of his Amherst students, and made them aware of those issues in contemporary life which seemed to him important. He had attractive theories about education, but he was handicapped by his inability or his unwillingness to see that an idea, to function at all, must function through human beings as they are at the moment.

I set down this description of him in no unfriendly spirit, but rather with the wish to explain his Amherst adventure. When the Trustees offered him the presidency they were asking him to meet a situation with which he was not familiar, and which they perhaps did not entirely understand. That a man of great personal charm and high ideals should not succeed in one of the most attractive of American colleges has puzzled, and continues to puzzle, all friends of Amherst. Students who came under the spell of his winning personality are still loyal to him, and feel that he suffered from the Trustees a serious injustice, but they cannot say what the injustice was.

It may be that neither these alumni nor the Trustees ever understood Amherst history as I have tried to describe it in the preceding chapter. Without such understanding the Meiklejohn episode is unintelligible. And unfortunately some parallel of the episode is likely to recur whenever a new president comes into an academic community without a keen awareness of its peculiar past.

Dr. Meiklejohns' estimate of the faculty situation at Amherst was at least two-thirds right. Any other new president would probably have agreed with him. There was too large a turnover in the youngest group of professors. Practically none of them was taking root in Amherst. Unless at least a majority of them became permanent fixtures, there could be no tradition in the College—no such tradition as the elder generation of the faculty had maintained through their active years. Though some of these elders were still teaching, it was easy for a new arrival to assume that their influence was shrinking, that their day was past, and that the sooner they were retired the more room there would be for new, and presumably excellent, youngsters.

The central group of the Amherst faculty were on the whole not productive. Few teachers of Greek, for example, were abler or better equipped than Harry deForest Smith, or few teachers of mathematics abler or more devoted than George Olds, but neither of these men published anything in his subject. That is, neither shared the fruits of his researches with other teachers of his subject, and therefore neither exerted much influence outside of Amherst.

Dr. Meiklejohn, as I think, appraised correctly the problem in the youngest group and the middle group of his faculty. His mistakes were in the remedies he proposed. He underestimated the importance of the elder teachers, those who survived from the years when the College had become famous. He ignored entirely the fact that public opinion in the little township would take the side of the elder generation and of the middle group in any clash which rose between them and a new and young president, a stranger.

A teacher, no matter how brilliant, if he becomes a college president, must become at once an educator. The college-president type of educator must be a statesman. His academic success, even his tenure of office, will depend less on the board of trustees than on the total good will of the community in which he has cast his lot. The fatal temptation for the novice is to adopt short-cut solutions. Any faculty at any time will contain some old teachers as well as some middle-aged and some young. It will contain also some good teachers and some less good. A resolute cutter of Gordian knots wants to retire at once all those teachers whom he wouldn't invite if he were starting fresh. In their place what can be simpler than to call new teachers, the very best? If other institutions are competing for them, then what is more obvious than to offer high salaries, even if untried youngsters are started off at almost twice the salary the veteran teachers have received all their lives? But the old teachers were once young, they once did good work, and having spent their lives in the community they have won without reservation the respect and affection of their neighbors. These neighbors are also growing old, they don't yet know the new president, they are watching him critically, they are looking for him to make a mistake.

Obviously, before he performs any major operation on his faculty, a new president should prove to the community, even to the nonacademic neighbors, that he deserves their respect and support. He who neglects this wisdom must hope to live in a vacuum. In the village of Amherst, at least, this cannot be done.

Furthermore, a new president had better earn quickly the respect and support of his elder teachers, those who even without his intervention will soon retire automatically. Their good opinion and their good wishes spread quickly among the non-academic neighbors, who henceforth accept the new president because the elders of the faculty believe in him.

If the middle-aged among the teachers are no longer what they should be, a reckless innovator may dismiss them, but in so doing he informs the world that he is not a great teacher, certainly not a competent leader. In war an army often deteriorates, loses its discipline and its morale. In such cases the soldiers are not sent home; the general is. The commander who knows his business, restores discipline and builds up morale. A college president is either this type of leader or he should not be president at all.

Of course the general can't train others to be first-rate soldiers unless he is a first-rate soldier himself. A college president cannot take in hand a lackadaisical faculty and reawaken in them one by one the scholarly flame, unless he is himself a flaming scholar.

2

In the spring of 1913 the Amherst chapter of Phi Beta Kappa invited me to deliver the address at their annual meeting. I was glad to see my old colleagues again, and to meet the new president, then finishing out his first year. The address which I read became later the first chapter of my book, *The Moral Obligation to be Intelligent.* The President of the society that season was Professor Emerson, who amused me by the precautions he took to guard against his famous absent-mindedness. As I sat beside him on the platform waiting for the exercises to begin, I saw that he kept before him, on a large sheet of paper, my name in immense block letters with arrows pointing toward it from the four corners of the page.

Seated among the faculty was Dr. Meiklejohn, alert, cordial, bubbling with energy. From that evening dated my friendship with him, and I suppose his wish to persuade me, if possible, to accept a call back to Amherst.[1] I could easily understand from this first contact why the Amherst boys gave him their allegiance practically at sight. He understood youth, and instinctively appealed to it.

Toward midnight that evening I was talking with Professor Bigelow, of the Music department, and deForest Smith, the Greek Professor, James Crook, Professor of Economics, and one or two others, in Fritz Thompson's study, where for years we had exchanged our best ideas and enjoyed Fritz's immense and tireless hospitality. I asked how the new President was getting on. Crook reserved judgment. Biggie was flatly against him, which was easy enough to understand since Dr. Meiklejohn cared little for music and did not realize the importance of the subject in modern education. De Forest Smith doubted if Meiklejohn understood either the College or the town. It was like deForest to see the problem to its depth. Fritz Thompson, wise and fair-minded as ever, spoke up for the new President, saying that the faculty, himself included, had got into a rut, and he believed Meiklejohn would get them out of it. Obviously he expected the kind of collaborating and companionable leadership by which a good general maintains the quality of his troops.

Then deForest gave a more precise judgment. Meiklejohn had started off on the wrong foot, and the error would prove fatal. On several occasions the new President had prophesied that Amherst would shortly have a first-rate faculty, equal man for man to the best group of teachers anywhere. DeForest's criticism was that when Meiklejohn said that Amherst would have a first-rate faculty, it sounded as though he said Amherst would *at last* have a first-rate faculty, forgetting the famous elders and all the devoted years of the middle-aged. The newcomer had publicly implied that until his own recent arrival, Amherst had never enjoyed an intellectual life worth remembering. Many of the alumni and most of the townspeople had caught this side-swipe, and were privately whetting their

[1] *The Memory*, p. 230.

knives. The survivors of the great era, Emerson, Elijah Harris, Anson Morse, and Genung, were of a calibre too magnificent to do any knife-whetting, but their dignified silence was understood.

DeForest concluded somewhat after this fashion: A new college president commits suicide if he speaks disparagingly of the older teachers, or of those who preceded them. By that approach he rouses enmities to himself which cannot be outweighed by undergraduate admiration. When undergraduates grow up, as in time they will, they learn that in any job a man must treat his associates with courtesy and respect. If he disagrees with them, he must convert without insulting them, no matter how annoying they are. He cannot remove them from the landscape. If he could, he would be not an educator, but an executioner; and when a college president gets himself a hangman's reputation, he might as well pack his trunk.

From this and other conversations with my old friends, I concluded that on the whole they agreed with Meiklejohn's criticisms, they were big enough to criticize themselves. The same could be said of the Trustees, the older alumni, the townspeople. If the patience of each group had come to an end at a different moment, Mr. Meiklejohn might have stayed. But early in 1923, in a queer fit of self-immolation, he got on the nerves of them all at the same time. I shall deal somewhat with that exchange of compliments in the next chapter.

3

In July, 1915, after I had declined Mr. Meiklejohn's invitation to return to Amherst, he asked me to name an English teacher to take my place. In spite of what I knew and thought about the Amherst situation, it seemed fair to tell him that the man I wanted at Columbia was Stuart P. Sherman, then at the University of Illinois. Meiklejohn at once got in touch with Stuart, who wrote me a little series of revealing letters, in which the disadvantages of a country college are touched on.

July 22, 1915.

My dear Erskine:

President Meiklejohn has asked me to go to Amherst under conditions similar to what he has been recently proposing to you. He tells me that you have resisted quietly all his allurements, and he also says that you raised certain objections, and that I may write you and ask what they are.

I have written to him that the Illinois people will not allow the decision to turn on pecuniary considerations, and that my decision will rest primarily on these two points. First, whether I should be blackballed and ostracized by other members of the faculty as an overpaid interloper; and second, whether the position would actually allow the holder a good wide margin for private occupations, that is, study and writing, after he has satisfied expectations as teacher and "educator."

If you are willing at this time to earn my everlasting gratitude, you will write me a brutally frank note on the first point in particular, and you will add all the other "buts" you can think of. Mr. Meiklejohn, whom I like very much, is a very poor hand at painting the defects of the position. I said to him very boldly in our conversation in Chicago that, if he brought in a man at a salary so far above the average, he might expect to touch rather deeply the exquisite jealousies of the professorial mind. And I can't recall now that he answered the objection.

I shall be grateful for your note whatever its tenor. For I am not in the least anxious to leave Illinois, where every one has been very friendly, and all sorts of new enterprises are humming. The hope of a quieter leisure for writing is the positive pull. And the apprehension of wounded sensibilities in Amherst is at present the chief negative force. If that is to be expected in any measurable degree, the attractions of Illinois resume their interrupted sway, and the Amherst scale flies heavenwards!

I have seen with delight Bourne's rapt picture of you in the *New Republic*. But don't you rather resent the way he lengthens out the foreground so that you stand in your serene and mellow age, surrounded by the golden glamour of antiquity?

Sincerely yours,
Stuart P. Sherman

I answered that a newcomer on the Amherst faculty would hardly be popular no matter how much the older professors admired him, if his salary were much more than theirs. I said this knowing the increasing sensitiveness at Amherst over the changes Dr. Meiklejohn contemplated, but I was not yet aware that he had offered Stuart $5,000 a year, whereas the oldest and most distinguished of the faculty had no more than $3,000. What he intended to give me if I resumed my work at Amherst, I don't know, since he never raised the question of salary.

Of course I could hardly plead the advantages of Amherst, since I had recently left it for Columbia, but I could sincerely point out the charm of the place, the friendly companionship to be found there, the leisurely opportunities for writing. Sherman at that time occupied a remarkable position as philosopher of American life and literature, and I knew he could make use of more leisure for writing than he could find at Urbana. Further, I called his attention to the few hours needed to reach either Boston or New York from Amherst.

On August third he wrote me that he had decided not to leave the University of Illinois. One paragraph of the letter drove hard at the question of the small college versus the large university. But he put the question correctly, not as a matter of size but of location. An educational institution, even though it begins in a small place, will soon be a large college or even a university if it has the qualities to attract students, especially mature students. In a world where education is much sought after, the college which remains small has much to explain. Here is what Stuart said about it, speaking of the faculty:

> The problem at Amherst, or one of them, is to get enough good men together to keep one another company. I fancy Meiklejohn will solve it, if anyone can. I was not quite convinced that one wouldn't be in a certain sense less companioned there than here. Our crowd is big enough here always to contain some men you would like to talk with if you and they had time. It isn't an altogether solid argument, on the other hand, to say that Amherst is within a few hours' ride of Boston and New York; so is Urbana! If I ever move now it will be to some place which I am persuaded is heaven and not one of its suburbs.

For both Stuart and me there was some unexpressed humor or irony in this correspondence. The head of the department at Illinois had been Professor Raymond M. Alden, who in 1914 accepted a professorship at Stanford University. On January 23, 1915, six months before the exchange of letters over the Amherst invitation, Stuart wrote me asking whether I should be interested in succeeding Alden as head of the department at Illinois. He did not wish an executive post himself, but President James laid upon him the burden of finding an executive. I quote his letter to me because of the picture he draws of the English department at Illinois, and because of the reservations and implications he makes about the advantage of a teacher's life in one place rather than in another.

My dear Erskine:

You very likely know that the vacancy made last year in our department by the resignation of R. M. Alden has not been filled. The task of finding a suitable man to supply the void has fallen more or less into my hands. Of course when the University seeks a professor, it wants the best available man in the country. In addition to this general prerequisite, there are certain specific and departmental qualifications which I urge as occasion offers.

We need a man who is a first-rate human being, a recognized scholar, a successful teacher of graduate and undergraduate students, and not inexperienced in the general problems of a large department. In my opinion the most useful man for us will be one engaged in literature rather than in language. And I have found that the most stimulating teachers of literature are those who write with adequate scientific and historical curiosity [and with] considered [considerable?] aesthetic and philosophic interest. Since we have already a tolerable group of Anglo-Saxon and Middle English scholars, our new man should preferably occupy some field from the Renaissance down. Among our conspicuous "openings" may be mentioned the literature of the Renaissance comparatively considered; poetics and the history of poetry, and the history of fiction.

If you have read the preceding paragraph with due attention, you have probably seen in it a partial portrait of yourself. Since you are at present, so far as one can see, in the plain pathway of academic prosperity, I suppose it is absurd to think of disengaging you even temporarily from Columbia. However: as I do not wish to approach any one who is *not* in the pathway of academic prosperity, I am ready to risk absurdly small chances. To tell the truth, I don't know how to get you off my mind, except by asking you flatly whether you would be willing to be considered a candidate for any kind of position that we could offer you in the department of English.

For just the right man we should try to make this position as attractive as such a position can be made in this part of the world. You will understand well enough at what points we could and at what points we could not compete with, say,—Harvard.

I answered promptly that my work at Columbia was opening up happily, and I had no intention of making a change, even to accept the great compliment Stuart suggested. In my reply I made some reference to our fast-growing friendship, the similarity of our ideals in teaching, and the pleasure I was having in our collaboration on the *Cambridge History of English Literature.* I added my hope that some day he might join me at Columbia, which I was quite sure would prove not a suburb of heaven, but the place itself.

After Sherman declined the Amherst call, Mr. Meiklejohn asked for other suggestions, and we had a rather animated discussion about the disadvantage of the country college when it competed with the large university for the brightest young men, fresh from their graduate work. I believed, judging from my own experience, that they would come to Amherst gladly, but in a few years they would be drawn back to the city.

Looking over our exchange of letters, after thirty years, I feel the warmest admiration for the courtesy and the good humor with which he maintained his side of the argument, refusing to admit that the country college is handicapped by its location, or that Amherst college in particular suffered from anything but a lack of the right teachers. I can see now that I failed him by not being entirely frank. His own courtesy made it difficult or impossible to remind him of his shortcomings as a leader and as a scholar. It would always be easier for him to dismiss an unsatisfactory teacher than to improve him; and whatever may have been his acquaintance in other fields of study, in English he was helpless. He did not know who were the promising youngsters, nor where to look for them.

In a letter dated April 15, 1915, he wrote that he had not forgotten my suggestion for a summer school at Amherst. He never mentioned the plan again. It was a scheme to bring first-rate youngsters to Amherst, where he could look them over. The session would be for four weeks, and the faculty would be four top-flight scholars, all in the same field. One year the subject would be history, another year mathematics, another year economics, etc. Each professor would give a lecture on Tuesday and another on Thursday. If there were two lecture periods in the mornings and afternoons of Tuesdays and Thursdays, a student could if he wished follow the courses of all four scholars.

Each Wednesday morning one of the scholars would lay before his colleagues, in the presence of the students, the particular investigation or research which had his attention just then. Criticism and discussion would follow in an extended forum, or later in informal consultations with the speaker of the day.

The students would be drawn, I hoped, from the younger ranks of college or school teachers, and from the graduate schools. If the scholars were sufficiently outstanding, no young teacher could afford to miss the opportunity of hearing and consulting the masters in his subject.

In 1915, when living was inexpensive, it was easy to suggest a budget for this four-week session. The charge to each student would be $100, for all the lectures and for a room in the dormitories. The visiting professors would be the guests of the College; each would receive $2,000. Each would be asked in advance to give the Librarian a list of the books he would need, and if these books were not already in the Library, they would be promptly bought.

I pointed out to Mr. Meiklejohn that such a summer school would simplify his search for young teachers. If he were in need of a geologist or a physicist, he would simply devote the next summer to geology or physics, secure the leaders in the subject to lecture, advertise the session among all the youngsters in the subject, and wait quietly in Amherst until they poured in. After looking them over, he could pick what he wanted, and meanwhile the Library would be improved with volumes selected by experts.

I thought out this plan for other reasons over and beyond my wish to help Mr. Meiklejohn. During my six Amherst years I was troubled by the fact that for almost four months out of twelve the dormitories and the classrooms were empty. For one third of the time the whole college passed out, like the Sleeping Beauty in the fairy tale. I believe this summer slumber still occurs in certain colleges, but the best follow the example of the universities and stay awake all year. A few, like the city universities, serve the community at night as well as during the day.

I was helpful to Mr. Meiklejohn only in the continued suggestion of individual teachers for him to entice to Amherst if he could. On September 9, 1915, he wrote to thank me for George Whicher and for Stark Young. Whicher had been an Amherst pupil of mine and had taken his Ph.D. at Columbia. Stark Young, a Columbia M.A., was Professor of English at the University of Texas, but through Professor Trent I knew that he wanted to come North. After six years he gave up his Amherst professorship for editorial work on the *New Republic* and the *Theatre Arts Monthly*. Then in addition to dramatic criticism he undertook the writing of plays and fiction, notably *So Red the Rose*.

George Whicher has long been the head of the English department at Amherst, a fine scholar, an able and prolific writer, a first-rate teacher. He alone, if my memory does not slip, remains of all the improvements Mr. Meiklejohn tried to plant in the Amherst I knew; and George Whicher was a product of that Amherst.

CHAPTER VI

Teaching at Amherst Again

1

O N MARCH 27, 1923, Edward T. Esty, the Secretary of the Amherst Trustees, wrote that the Board had voted to confer on me the degree of Litt. Dr. if I would be present to receive it in Amherst on Commencement Day, June twentieth. Naturally I was pleased that the College where I had begun my teaching wished to give me this honor twenty years after I had first joined its faculty. Through the spring months I thought often of my coming visit and planned to go up a few days before Commencement for long, quiet talks with my old friends.

Just what had been happening to the College since 1915 I knew but vaguely. The war had interrupted whatever plans President Meiklejohn had inaugurated for the new and greater Amherst. My old colleague Robert Utter had been with me at Beaune, serving as Chairman of the English department there. Fritz Thompson, the historian, had worked in the French *Foyers du Soldat,* and Bill Newlin, mathematician and philosopher, one of the original group in Mrs. Marsh's house, had come to France with the Y.M.C.A. and had joined us at Beaune. Dean Woodbridge I knew had become an extremely active member of the Amherst Trustee Board. With Dwight Morrow, his close friend, he did all he could as soon as peace returned to strengthen Mr. Meiklejohn's hand and to promote the welfare of the College, which both he and Morrow loved with a youthful, almost fanatic, adoration. Even during the war, and still more immediately afterward, Dwight made the College handsome gifts of dormitories and other benefactions. The campus was changing fast and, as most people would feel, for the better, but I, prejudiced in favor of the times I had known, regretted the disappearance of Mrs. Davis's house where we had sat at the well-known table. Undoubtedly the handsome fraternity building which re placed it was 'an architectural improvement, but something had gone from the village charm. The new Library, on the site of Hitchcock Hall, commodious, modern, and convenient, was very much like any first-rate library building. In my heart I preferred the gaunt structure on the other side of the Common where my students and I had satisfied our thirst for sound learning.

There were changes on the faculty and at least one important addition. From 1916 to 1920, Robert Frost, the poet, had been teaching at Amherst on an intermittent professorship which the College would have been glad to make full time if Frost had not wished to keep himself free for his poetry. Just who brought him to Amherst, I don't know, but I suspect it was Dwight Morrow. I suspect also that Dwight provided the funds to bring him.

Frost then was, as he still is, an original and fascinating talker, something of a genius as a teacher, vaguely unhappy when he doesn't hold a teaching job, and still more unhappy when he does. He once told me that he was like the monkey fascinated by the snake, the snake being the teaching profession. He knew that its neighborhood wasn't good for him, yet he couldn't stay away. In spite of this excess of temperament, I think he should have accepted teaching as one of his obligations to society. Other writers are always stimulated by his ideals and his wise comments on the art of writing, and for young students he can be an amazing inspiration.

As June twentieth drew nearer, I learned that Frost was once more taking up his teaching at Amherst, and this time quite certainly because Woodbridge and Dwight Morrow thought the College needed him badly. The relations between the faculty and the President had deteriorated. Also the relations between the President and the alumni. Also, his relations with the Trustees. Also, and most unfortunately, his relations with the townsfolk. The principles of human relations which I have already described were beginning to work with full force and at top speed. The Amherst students were on the whole devoted to the President, and to most if not all of the teachers he had brought in, but the students in previous generations had also been devoted to their teachers, or at least to the best of them, and they were still loyal. When they learned, as in time they did, that Mr. Meiklejohn did not think highly of the teachers to whom they were grateful, their enmity was assured. Among the Amherst townsfolk the same principle operated. It was a calamity for Mr. Meiklejohn that without intending to do so he made clear his low opinion of teachers whom the town had a hundred good reasons for honoring.

On what occasion he happened just then to rouse his critics among the townsfolk, I do not know, but I heard much from my friends on the faculty of his maladroit handling of them and the Trustees. He had conveyed once too often the impression that he did not take seriously either his senior professors or the governing board of the College. By disregarding them, he seemed to imply that they could be dispensed with.

The incident which developed into the final crisis concerned a young teacher whom Mr. Meiklejohn—and the rest of the faculty—admired. When he had taught at the College a year, or slightly more, Mr. Meiklejohn recommended him to the Educational Committee of the Trustees for promotion. One of the Committee asked a routine question. "Do his colleagues in the department approve of this recommendation?"

Mr. Meiklejohn replied that they did not. They approved thoroughly of the young man's work, but doubted whether he had as yet earned the promotion. Their wish was that he should first teach for another year. Mr. Meiklejohn felt that since he had already proved his quality, he should be promoted at once.

The Committee told the President that they declined to umpire any dispute between him and his professors. He must agree with them or persuade them to agree with him.

If I remember the story correctly, Mr. Meiklejohn a month later recommended the promotion again before a meeting of the entire Trustee Board, and when questioned rather sharply admitted that the department did not yet endorse the recommendation, and that the Committee at the preliminary meeting had advised him not to bring before them for adjudication his differences of opinion with his faculty. The recommendation was laid on the table.

A year later the departmental colleagues were entirely willing to recommend the promotion, and Mr. Meiklejohn, sure of their attitude, neglected to go through the form of asking for their approval. When he presented the case to the Educational Committee, they wanted to know if the faculty now approved, and he took a chance and said they did—meaning they probably would if and when he asked them.

A few days later it occurred to him that he should get the approval of the faculty on record. Calling the department together, he told them that he wished to present the nomination, but not that he had already presented it. The professors voted to approve, and spent the rest of the evening discussing with the President some other subject. In the course of the discussion a disagreement occurred, which a few days later one of the group mentioned to a member of the Trustee Educational Committee.

"When did this debate take place?" asked the Trustee.

"The evening last week when we met to approve So-and-So's promotion."

The Trustee turned red in the face. "But *that* recommendation was brought to us with your endorsement more than a week ago!"

From that time on tempers were lost and the fur flew. Professors and Trustees felt that the President had been making fools of them.

The precise truth of this story in all details I can not vouch for, but I believe it because of my own adventures with Mr. Meiklejohn. His kind intentions I never doubted, but, to say the least, he was incurably unbusinesslike, and without wishing to do so, he usually conveyed the impression that he did not take the other man seriously. I have told elsewhere that in a fashion he invited me back to Amherst. He had already asked me face to face whether I would consider returning. I had answered that I would not. He then telephoned from Amherst one morning, asking me to catch a train within the hour and hurry up for a conference on the future of his English department. I said at once, "I hope this does not mean you wish to invite me again. I appreciate the compliment, of course, but I shall remain at Columbia."

"That's not what I wish to talk about," he replied. "I want advice about the department."

By traveling all day, I reached his home in the early evening. As soon as we were alone, his first words were, "Tell me some reasons why you should not return to Amherst!"

My emotions are easy to guess. I was angry that he had made free with my time under false pretenses. Later, when my indignation had subsided, I was amused that not once in his flattering but embarrassing attempts to dislodge me from Columbia, had he thought it worth while to mention the conditions under which Amherst wanted me. He never mentioned my duties nor what my salary would be. Very subtly his silence on such matters suggested that no high-minded gentleman would ever think of them. If he practiced the same noble philosophy in his dealings with the Amherst townspeople, I can understand their lack of enthusiasm.

Pity that American education does not provide a course in human relations for prospective college heads, nor a course for Trustees on How to Pick a President!

2

The atmosphere of the quiet little college in June, 1923, was more embattled than anything I had known in the war. When I took the train for Amherst on the seventeenth the New York papers reported without excessive emphasis that the long feud between the President and his Trustees was becoming serious. At Hartford the evening papers gave more space to the story, with a hint that the President might resign before long. At Springfield the newspapers were so alarming that I abandoned the idea of proceeding to Fritz Thompson's house, where I was to be a guest. Instead I went to a Springfield hotel and telephoned Fritz that I would appear just in time to take my degree. I wondered whether the excited little college would cool off sufficiently to hand out any degrees that season.

The Commencement was held, nevertheless, and arriving half an hour before the ceremonies, I learned that Mr. Meiklejohn's resignation had been accepted, that practically all the teachers he had brought to Amherst had resigned, and that the seniors who were most loyal to him had announced their intention of throwing their diplomas back in the face of Amherst College, if Amherst College insulted them by offering its contemptible sheepskin.

In a few minutes the academic procession formed, we marched to the College Hall, and the tragic orgy began. Mr. Meiklejohn was a pathetic figure, obviously worn out and in need of sleep. Whatever mistakes he had made or was still to make, everyone in the crowded room remembered his fine record as a teacher, the excellent ideals of education which he would have realized if he had known how, and the devotion of the undergraduates. No educator ever wins the warm approval of youth without from some point of view deserving it.

The College Hall was jammed with students, with the relatives of the graduating class, with alumni, with townsfolk, and with a number of reporters from near-by towns and from distant cities. We all expected, or feared, an explosion, and it came when Mr. Meiklejohn conferred the first diploma. The recipient handed it back with a nervous and jejune statement about the unworthiness of Alma Mater to bestow honors that morning. After a second diploma had been returned, Mr. Meiklejohn asked the remainder of the class not to come up on the platform unless it was their intention to accept their diplomas. The class stayed in their seats, and the graduation ceremonies were quickly over.

Everything worked against poor Mr. Meiklejohn that morning. This diploma incident angered the alumni, who were already his critics. They had heard that the seniors had told Mr. Meiklejohn in advance that they would hand back their diplomas. They had heard also that he had tried to make them change their minds. Alumni judgment of the incident was that if he had been educating these boys for four years, he should have taught them a little common sense and an instinctive reluctance to attack their college and to discredit it in public. What the boys had learned from him, apparently, was that he and his opinions were more precious than Amherst College, or its past, or its future.

To turn the diploma incident into a criticism of the retiring President may have been natural, but in my opinion it was unfair. The critics had not gone through all the worries and perplexities which, whether or not he himself was to blame, almost broke down Mr. Meiklejohn's health. In his handling of his youthful followers that Commencement morning he was not wise, but I wonder if any who disagreed with him could under such pressure be wiser.

The students recovered their equanimity as soon as the bestowal of honorary degrees began. Each guest was applauded with the usual courtesy. For me Mr. Meiklejohn had prepared a generous laureation, a salute which would have given me happiness if I could have heard the words from him in circumstances agreeable to both of us. As it was, the experience was more than a little ghastly, and like many others who were present I left the College Hall much troubled for Amherst, and to a certain extent for education in America.

But the drama was not yet over. At the alumni luncheon Mr. Meiklejohn took his farewell of Amherst in a spirited defense of himself and an attack on all whom he blamed for his difficulties. It was a brilliant speech but marvelously unwise. He expressed in plain terms his worst opinions of the faculty, of the Trustees, and of the alumni. His admiration he reserved exclusively for the students who applauded his praise of them, and perhaps would have cheered vigorously if he hadn't assaulted the alumni. Undergraduates are usually on good terms with the graduates, especially with the older members of the fraternities who help the youngsters keep the fraternity houses going. Perhaps the undergraduates were also beginning to doubt the wisdom of the diploma incident. An Amherst student is out of his element if he isn't cheering for the College.

I was scheduled to speak at the alumni luncheon, following Mr. Meiklejohn. I had prepared my speech carefully and had memorized it. Since it expressed my philosophy as well as anything I could invent in the excitement of the moment, I delivered it unaltered.

I spoke in almost complete silence. The alumni were surprised, perhaps, that I didn't reply to Mr. Meiklejohn, point by point; the younger generation probably set me down for a self-confessed back number. But I had come to the Commencement festivities to declare my affection for the College, and I held to that purpose—in words later published in the *Amherst Graduates' Quarterly* (November, 1923).

3

The resignation of Mr. Meiklejohn and most of his young teachers gave the College a problem. The Trustees immediately elected as the next president Dean George D. Olds, whose popularity with the remaining faculty members, and with the alumni and with the town, helped at once to restore morale. But something had been lost which was not easy to recover. The antagonism between faculty and President during the administration so abruptly ended, had left the professors in a chastened and rather discouraged mood. It was no cause of pride that Mr. Meiklejohn had underestimated their quality, or that they had not felt able to give him their support. As a group my former colleagues were exhausted. Though they had won the ungracious struggle, it had left them flat on their backs. Perhaps in their hearts they suspected that their long satisfaction with their easygoing life justified at least in part Mr. Meiklejohn's wish to replace them with younger and more active scholars. The withdrawal of the new men whom he had brought in, put them on the spot. It was now their turn to take the lead, but on the whole they had neither the energy nor the ideas to strike out in any new direction.

This memory of them at that moment rests on talks with Professor Bigelow, with deForest Smith, Fritz Thompson, and Charles Cobb, old friends for whose clear heads and sense of fairness I had unlimited respect. President Olds himself spoke freely of his age, saying he could hope only to hold the College together for a while until it could catch its breath.

With the aid of Dwight Morrow and of Woodbridge, he made a temporary arrangement with Columbia to borrow teachers for part-time service. In the second half of 1923-1924 I gave two courses weekly at Amherst, going up at noon on Fridays to hold a seminar in the evening, giving a large lecture course Saturday morning, and returning Saturday afternoon. On these trips my companion was a close friend, Lindsay Rogers, Burgess Professor of Public Law at Columbia. We spent Friday nights in one of the new dormitories, and had opportunities to talk with the students as well as with the other teachers, and on the train coming back we compared notes.

We agreed that during the Meiklejohn regime the students had been trained to unusual skill in debate. Some of them were masters of dialectic. They could and did argue on the basis of little information, or none at all, and their keenness of mind, strange to say, had nothing to do with intellectual curiosity. When Rogers and I, in our different subjects, began to require thorough reading and systematic study, the boys were on the whole courteous, even docile, but they continued to prefer glibness to knowledge, and the complacency with which they acknowledged their bad habits, was baffling. Once they understood their case they enjoyed talking about it, but they had small wish to cure it.

Late one Friday night, at the close of my seminar, I accepted an invitation to meet a group of students in a dormitory room—charming boys, all of them.

"Professor, you seem to think we are intellectually lazy."

I admitted I thought so.

The boys smiled happily. "Professor, that's just what we are! We don't study enough. We don't read enough. What we wish to ask you, Professor, is just how that condition can be improved."

They were eager for my reply, poised to tear me to pieces with their facile and nimble logic. Their complacency, their lack of seriousness, was exasperating.

"Perhaps nothing can be done for you, since your trouble begins with your legs."

They looked up, startled.

"The Library is next door, the reading room is not a hundred feet from where we are sitting; to get there you have only to walk. Apparently none of you can walk in that direction, and I doubt if the College will bring the Library to you."

They didn't mind my teasing, and before the spring term was over both Lindsay Rogers and I thought we noticed symptoms of awakening ambition here and there, but they still were terrible talkers, keeping themselves alive on whatever sustenance can be drawn from hot air.

Amherst as I had first known it was gone. Around the village Common had sprung up handsome new fraternity houses. Mrs. Baxter Marsh still rented rooms to faculty bachelors, but a new house had gone up on the vacant lot which formerly gave my study windows their sunlight and their wide view. Bigelow with his pianos was installed in the old Octagon, since the new Library had driven him out of Hitchcock Hall. Charles Cobb and one or two others now preferred to live quite out of the village; Charles had a room at the Golf Club south of the Boston and Maine station. Martha Bianchi still lived on Maine Street in her father's house, and still welcomed guests in the little study with the magazine-covered table, the book-lined walls, and the friendly fireplace. But her mother was dead, and I missed the wit and the searching ideas of the much-debated Susan. My old memories were badly disarranged.

Yet the Amherst landscape exerted its old magic, especially as the spring came on. There were many moments when I forgot the limitations and the handicaps of a country college and began to dream again of what might be accomplished by the right teachers in a spot so poetic, so inspiring, so removed from the noisy interruptions of city life. Gradually an educational program suggested itself which would make of Amherst something more than a college. Not a university, not even a country university, but a traditional American college enriched with a new kind of advanced study.

Each department might take care of a few specially able boys without increasing the number of teachers. I imagined how I would organize the English work if I were now teaching in Amherst. From the freshman class I would select the students, probably not more than one or two, who had a special flair for literature and for writing. By private encouragement and coaching I would guide their reading so that by the time they had their diplomas they would be as widely read as most of the university candidates for a Ph.D. Since Amherst's charter permits the giving of an M.A., I would keep these special students for an extra year so that they might read still more and incidentally receive from me some training in the art of teaching. They would handle a few sections of the freshman and sophomore classes, and I would watch and criticize their work. When they took their M.A. they would be better scholars and better teachers than most graduate schools can produce. If I found one or two boys of the right quality in each class, I was sure I could place them in good positions as soon as they had their Master's degree. If ever they wanted a Ph.D., they could go to a university and get it, though I would advise them against the waste of time.

This plan could be followed by the other professors in their subjects. The atmosphere of the College would become more intellectual, the scholarly ambitions of the teachers would be revived and exercised.

I laid this program before Dean Woodbridge in a long letter which he showed to Dwight Morrow, and we three spent a long and pleasant evening discussing it on Tom Lamont's yacht up the Hudson as far as Poughkeepise, and for the rest of the night at Dwight's home in Morristown. Either Dwight or Woodbridge reported it to the Amherst faculty through President Olds, and on my week-end visits for the rest of the year I began to get surprising comments—which after all ought not to have surprised me.

President Olds, straight-thinking and friendly, told me at once once that he liked the plan but it wouldn't be acceptable to the faculty, and since he couldn't convert them by his example, he would not try to persuade them by argument. In order to train young scholars and teachers by the kind of tutorial system I was proposing, every professor would have to set an example in study and research, would have to teach his whole subject rather than a special corner of it, and would have to be a model of pedagogy in the classroom. On one condition the President would adopt the plan as his own and try his best to win over the faculty. He would hope for success, he said, if I came back to Amherst and installed the program in the English department. He promised me a free hand, an adequate salary, any addition I wanted to the resources of the Library. I had no doubt of the soundness of my own plan, and of its potential value to American education. President Olds may well have been restrained in his enthusiasm just because for years he had been accustomed to what an Amherst colleague once called my massive faith in my own ideas. But now I too was cautious. I said that if the faculty were opposed to the suggested program, I could not accept an invitation to try it out. President Olds countered with a compliment; if I returned and set up the new order in the English department, my colleagues, he believed, would eventually follow me. Eventually! I stayed at Columbia.

After talks that spring with Bigelow, deForest Smith and Fritz Thompson, I understood the dilemma I had posed for Amherst professors. By training and practice they could teach undergraduates, but they had not expected to be responsible for advanced courses, and they were not sure they wanted to make the experiment. Obviously the new program would call for hard work and other changes in their habits. Bigelow stood somewhat outside of the debate, since the study of music follows its own pattern, and his department was in those days decidedly in advance of what most universities were doing. But he saw the problem from all points of view, and helped me to understand Fritz and deForest.

"Are you trying to make a country university out of us? An Oxford, or at least a Princeton? If your plan should work, won't you put an end to the American small college?"

I disclaimed any intention or hope of turning Amherst into a university. That couldn't be done without the establishment of law and medical schools, and other schools to cover the universal range of knowledge. But I admitted that if my program or any other should make Amherst known for the unique value of its instruction, earnest students would flock in by the hundreds.

"And you see an advantage in numbers?"

"More students would call for a larger faculty," I answered, picking my steps through an awkward subject. "A more numerous faculty ought to give all the teachers a more congenial social life. There would be more points of view, more scholarly contacts, the moments of intellectual inspiration would be more frequent."

Dear Fritz Thompson, short, chubby and kind, who had a fine library but didn't read it, who would gladly build an extension of his shelves to hold the books his friends wrote, but who never got around to cutting the pages—Fritz, one of the most lovable friends I ever had, fixed an admonishing eye on me, and expressed the hope that a modicum of common sense might linger in me, and that I would not attempt to alter beyond recognition the world as God in his wisdom had made it.

Remembering my dreams for the little college on its lovely hill, and the nostalgic pull it exerted on me, as on many others, I give thanks for the beneficent fate which after each backward glance set me firmly again in the path that belonged to me. If my former colleagues had welcomed my plan for advanced instruction, I would have accepted the invitation of President Olds, I would have turned my back on Columbia, on the work at the Juilliard, on whatever else waited among the potentialities of New York life.

One Amherst graduate, a well-known educator, wrote to me somewhat later asking my permission to propose me as Mr. Meiklejohn's successor. He had gone to Europe after the Commencement of 1923, and so had missed the news of Dean Olds's election. For many years my reply to him gave me troubled hours whenever I happened to remember it. The tone of Amherst love in it might suggest that I should be open to a call whenever a vacancy occurred, to the end of time.

I explain to myself these fits of insane affection by watching the enchantment the Amherst landscape continues to lay upon others who for a while have lived with it. The spell is cast by the landscape, not by the College, and the magic would be no less if the College were only a good preparatory school, as at moments it has been.

In 1946 Lewis Perry retired as Principal of Phillips-Exeter Academy, the next year Claude Fuess, an Amherst student of mine, Principal of Phillips-Andover, announced his intention to retire, and Stanley King, in the same year, retired as President of Amherst College. The three retiring educators had brought their institutions magnificently through the ordeal of the Second World War. They laid down their responsibilities with relief we must suppose, and certainly with the admiring applause of all who understood the peril through which civilized culture in all Western lands had been passing. Yet the mood of gratitude did not prevent thoughtful educators from asking in what the historic College excelled the two historic preparatory schools except in the hypnotic influence of its landscape.

When the westering sun strikes the slopes of the Pelham Hills, especially in spring, especially when the orchards, blossoming in their proper colors, turn the hillsides into rioting checkerboards, the Amherst boys dream incurable dreams, and I can certify that a young instructor, through six springtimes, dreamed of a noble kind of education, in which, as in the heavenly ride of which Plato spoke, the wings of the soul might be nourished by the contemplation of eternal ideas.

That was almost forty years ago. The eternal ideas remain, but they challenge us in new ways. Remembering Amherst with lasting affection, I wish for it not the ivy-tower privilege of lost causes and forsaken loyalties. The critical age we live in will praise no more in the college than in the individual, a fugitive and cloistered virtue, unexercised and unbreathed.

CHAPTER VII

Teaching in a City University

1

WHEN I returned to Columbia in 1909 I soon found myself spending a good deal of time in the office of the Philosophy department on the top floor of Philosophy Hall, or in Professor Keyser's study on the ground floor of Hamilton Hall. In the Philosophy office, Frederick J. E. Woodbridge and Wendell T. Bush had their desks, and though Professor Bush's many non-curricular interests kept him out of the room except when he was editing the *Journal of Philosophy, Psychology and Scientific Method,* Professor Woodbridge, on the other hand, was always there, except when he was meeting his classes.

Wendell Bush was large and powerfully built, fond of horseback riding and of life in the open air. His brother, Irving T. Bush, created the Bush Terminal, New York City. The impression made by Wendell's powerful frame was balanced, or contradicted, by a nervous hesitation in his speech, by the gentleness of his manners, and by his fondness for painting and for music. The most generous and the most modest of men, he spent his considerable private income promoting the intellectual causes he loved and in making life easier for artists and scholars he believed in. Though he was a familiar and popular figure on the campus, I doubt if many of his colleagues except President Butler, Fred Woodbridge, and John Dewey knew how much the life of the University owed to him. Since he admired George Santayana, then still at Harvard, and Professor Gilbert Murray, of Oxford, those two unforgettable persons each gave at Columbia a course of lectures. Most of us did not know at the time that Santayana's course on *Three Philosophical Poets* and Gilbert Murray's lectures on *Four Stages of Greek Religion* were both provided by special gifts from Wendell Bush. If I am not mistaken the *Journal of Philosophy* frequently received financial aid from the same source.

His passion for music and art disclosed itself in intimate talks at the faculty house, or in his home. His tastes were so catholic and his curiosity so lively that I never could make up my mind whether he preferred classical art or modernistic experiment. Certainly he liked to give all kinds a fair chance. He owned many paintings by Arthur B. Davies; in fact, his apartment was a veritable Davies museum, and I owe to him my one opportunity to meet the painter, whom I too admired, but with reservations. At the moment the important American painter for me was George Bellows.

One night Bush brought Davies to an undergraduate discussion group, most of the students coming from his classes, Woodbridge's and mine. Davies told me afterward that he was disappointed at the apparent reluctance of the students to strike out in their opinions and be themselves, as he imagined they really were. Boys so young, he said, ought to be intoxicated with the future, aggressively so, but instead of being in love with their own opinions, our Columbia youngsters, he regretted to notice, had a tendency to be respectful and polite. I couldn't quarrel with his opinion, but the thought did occur to me that he himself was somewhat difficult in conversation, not at all the freely articulate spirit which he wished others to be, and was disappointed with the boys for not being. He was fairly tall, quite thin, and whatever is the opposite of robust. I think of him as refined and narrow, but since Bush admired him, he must have had qualities I didn't catch.

At a faculty luncheon one day Bush told me he had two tickets to the Beethoven sonata course which Harold Bauer and Jacques Thibaud were just then playing. There was a concert that afternoon. Would I come? Until that afternoon I did not know that Bush played the 'cello. The superb performance of the violin sonatas made him itch to get his fingers on the strings, and while we were applauding Bauer and Thibaud, he asked if I cared to go home with him and make some music of our own. In his apartment he got out his music and took off his coat, and we worked away at Beethoven sonatas until Mrs. Bush reminded him of a dinner engagement. The clock stood already at five minutes to eight.

Like everybody else who knew Frederick Woodbridge, I find it difficult to describe him. He inspired his colleagues as well as his students, and we all turned to him whenever our own supply of wisdom ran short. Yet he was not an energetic person in any sense which was clear to the eye, or which could be illustrated by an anecdote. He was, I believe, less tall than Bush but much heavier. I never knew a man so averse to exercise. Perhaps Dr. Samuel Johnson was his match. When Woodbridge finished with a class he would go back to his office, not to his desk but to his spacious easy chair, in which he recuperated from any expenditure of energy, even from writing a letter. Since he was a thoughtful man he had an equally capacious easy chair for guests to relax in.

How many times I have sunk into it with practically no disposition to get up again! Once he was settled, facing his caller, he would fill his pipe and reach for a match. He was a terrific smoker, consuming more matches perhaps than tobacco, and managing to burn a sad number of holes in his waistcoat or his coat. I once asked him why he had to drop so many sparks and match ends, or puff so many live coals from the bowl of his pipe. He replied that he didn't know why the damage was necessary, but it seemed to be.

He was devoted to Plato, not because he cared overmuch for the Platonic philosophy, but because the dialogues contain the portrait of Socrates, and Socrates was precisely the kind of man Woodbridge wanted us all to be—that is, all Columbia professors.

By temperament rather than by conscious imitation, he made himself, or at least he became, as much like Socrates as a modern man is likely to be. It happened that the tilt of his nose and the shape of his broad face suggested Xantippe's famous husband. Though the resemblance was accidental, Woodbridge took pleasure from the circumstance that Nature or Providence had provided his Socratic spirit with the right fleshly costume.

In 1909 and for several years after he gave an undergraduate course in the history of philosophy. Later this particular course for some reason was reserved for graduate students. The change was unfortunate. Either the philosophy of Plato or Woodbridge's way of interpreting Socrates had on the extremely youthful an extraordinary effect. Many of my own students took this course of his, and in their writing I could recognize the impact of his characteristic ideas. I was so fond of him and we were bound by so many strains of sentiment that it was a long time before I could study him and his philosophy with any degree of cool detachment.

For one thing, he was an Amherst graduate in the class of 1889, with my old friend William Bigelow, with Arthur Curtis James, the capitalist, whom I knew through Bigelow, and with Charles Seymour Whitman, who became District Attorney of my native city and Governor of the State. Whitman, I believe, had his Amherst diploma a year later than Woodbridge, Bigelow and James, but they were an inseparable quartet, and I remember them always associated in an Amherst atmosphere which perhaps their boyhood friendship created or revived when they met. Woodbridge and James were Amherst Trustees, long since tamed by heavy responsibilities, but Whitman and Bigelow, essentially untamable, both of them, overlooked in their comrades the handicap of dignity, substituting as far as possible a youthful joy of life.

Woodbridge was born in Canada, of British parentage, and though he gave his life to the study and teaching of Greek philosophy his character and his thinking may fairly be described as English to the core. He admired nothing so much as character and common sense, but it must be English character and English common sense. Hobbes was nearer to him than Plato, chiefly, or so it seemed to me, because Plato indulged in bold poetic flights, and neither flights nor poetry beguiled Hobbes from the geometrical path of his natural articulateness. Yet Woodbridge was drawn to poetry and Plato fascinated him—not quite the same Plato that I admired. Whenever I plunged into some enthusiastic praise of the *Symposium* or the *Phaedrus,* a puckering of his eyebrows warned me that we could spend the time more profitably on a less fanciful dialogue, one with less myth in it and more straight argument.

Woodbridge's influence upon all of us at Columbia, upon his students and his colleagues alike, was great indeed, but since few of his fellow teachers were sure what his philosophy was, it is fair to say that his influence reached us through his philosophy as transmuted into his extraordinary character. He was the most loyal and affectionate of friends, the most helpful and fair-minded of teachers; his academic and scholarly honors were high-lighted with a noble glow from the serene courage with which, in his closing years, he bore sorrow and pain. His wife, who had made his home very happy, went first, after a long and distressing illness. With no respite he learned immediately that he himself must endure a series of operations for the mere hope of surviving, a bedridden invalid, the rest of his days. But in spite of appalling handicaps he continued his studies, his teaching, his writing, and kept alive his warm friendships with his fellow scholars. From his bed he held court, as it were, for his affectionate visitors. The students of his seminars met at his bedside and continued their work under his guidance. His books were piled near his pillow within easy reach. To the end he clung to his pipe, lighting it incessantly, and dropping sparks on sheets and blankets as formerly on his waistcoat. We never heard him complain; as time went on his cheerfulness increased, or so it seemed to us. An additional visitor by his bedside always brought into his face an additional light.

A great man by any measure. At Columbia he is a cherished memory. Of his own wish he is buried in the cemetery at Amherst, the place where he was a student. His grave is near that of his friend Bigelow, and—he was always indifferent to local feuds—near the Dickinsons and the Todds, and not far from several of the great scholars who had been his teachers.

Since he loved Amherst, I never could understand why he did not accept the presidency of that college when it was offered to him, as on two occasions I believe it was—after the retirement of President Harris, and after the resignation of President Meiklejohn. The explanations which rumor supplied were for me rather silly. I heard that the Trustees on the earlier occasion feared that Woodbridge was too much of a rationalist, not sufficiently inspired with a warm Christian missionary spirit. I don't believe that a board looking for evangelical orthodoxy in their president, would have fixed on Mr. Meiklejohn.

When Woodbridge declined the opportunity for the second time, if indeed he did, I was told in Amherst that he felt Professor Olds deserved the post and should have had it long before. On the Columbia campus the explanation was that Woodbridge, having now devoted a number of years to the strengthening of the University Graduate School, thought it important to continue this work until such time as President Butler retired. The implication was that an invitation to be President of Columbia would not be declined.

But all this seems to me nonsense. Woodbridge was the least calculating of men. Whatever motives he had were surely unselfish and intelligent. I think he declined all presidencies because, although the administrative problems of education fascinated him, he was not an administrator. He was a philosopher rather than a man of action. He enjoyed thinking out the solution of a problem, but instinctively he backed away from the obligation to put his own remedies into effect. Even his comparatively minor duties as Dean of the Graduate School perplexed and preyed upon him; they interrupted his thoughts.

2

Cassius J. Keyser, Professor of Mathematics, was for me a particularly attractive kind of thinker, profound yet clear. Probably for the reason that I knew practically nothing of modern mathematical explorations into infinity, Keyser's ideas startled me with their novelty as well as their depth. But even beyond the clarity which one expects in a mathematician, Keyser had a genius for any kind of expression. In his youth he had played the violin, or as he called it, the fiddle, and in his frequent comments on language he unconsciously revealed the fact that he was blessed with a very musical ear. He was an orator by native gift and careful self-training. In this field he seemed to me superior to Woodbridge, who probably was, except for Keyser, our best speaker at Columbia. But clearness had always been my own ideal in writing and in speaking, and Keyser was the finest example of it I had met. He certainly did not seem to me less admirable because he shared my own worship of great French writers, those masters of clarity.

In fact, when I used to drop into Keyser's study for a talk, I often took to him a purely literary problem, certain of his interest and of his help. Practically everything I wrote in the years between 1910 and 1916 I read to Woodbridge and Keyser and had their comments before I showed it to anyone else. When I read Keyser my essay on "The Moral Obligation to be Intelligent" he at once asked for a copy for the *Hibbert Journal,* of which he was associate editor. Because I read the piece aloud in that book-lined little room at the west end of the Hamilton Hall corridor, it came about that my essay, originally prepared for Phi Beta Kappa ceremonies at Amherst, appeared first in a British publication. When Keyser asked for the manuscript, I told him that perhaps I was under some obligation to give it to the *Amherst Graduates' Quarterly,* the editor of which, said I hopefully, would no doubt ask for it. Keyser did not conceal his amusement at my confidence. He suggested there were things in my essay which might conceivably prevent some New England temperaments from admiring it. In case—just in case—the editor of the *Amherst Graduates' Quarterly* did not ask for the privilege of printing the speech, would I please remember that the associate editor of the *Hibbert Journal* was well disposed.

Keyser guessed right that time, as he usually did. When he sent the paper to the *Hibbert Journal,* Dr. Jacks published it at once. This incident was the first of many which made me realize that in returning to Columbia I had entered a large field of scholarship where unexpected opportunities were furnished almost daily by the sympathy and the wide influence of great colleagues.

Keyser, with his marked taste for the arts and his acquaintance with European culture, was a product of the Middle West. Born during the Civil War, he had grown up in Ohio and Missouri in a society which has not yet been made familiar by historians to American readers, and which Europeans usually insist on misunderstanding and misinterpreting. It was in more than one admirable sense a pioneer world. The creative spirit marked it in many ways, not least in its passion for education and for bold thinking. Keyser evidently came of a family in all respects typical of the region and the period. When he rose to speak in the faculty room, or when he exchanged ideas informally with his colleagues, most of them his younger colleagues, he always evoked for me a picture of society in the American West twenty years after the Civil War, when new towns were building, when the railroads were annihilating distance, when the purpose of public and private enterprise seemed to be a better preparation for a better world.

Keyser had an elder brother endowed with a fine mind and an obviously generous nature. This brother had worked for the family, postponing the things he had hoped to do for himself. Realizing at last that it was too late for him to secure the education he wished for, this brother came to Cassius one day with a considerable sum of money.

"I am too old," he said. "You take it, and make yourself what you should be."

Keyser told me the incident with much feeling. Perhaps his career was the result of a lifelong determination to justify the elder brother's faith. It seemed to me that he always assumed, or wished to assume, in our students the same heroic craving for knowledge which animated himself.

I write these words only a few weeks after Keyser's death at the age of eighty-five. His students and friends are preparing a complete edition of his writings. On my shelves I have two little books of his, one published in 1914, the other a year later. The first has the title *Science and Religion,* the second, *The New Infinite and the Old Theology.* I am tempted to quote the brief Preface to the earlier volume. It illustrates Keyser's quality of thought, almost the accent and certainly the spirit, of his conversation.

"The following address aims to suggest and to sketch a new way of thinking about old things of universal interest. The major emphasis falls upon the great function of Idealization regarded in the light of what mathematicians call the method or the process of Limits. The central thesis is that this process in the domain of reason or of rational thought indicates the reality, and, in part, the nature of a domain beyond, a realm super-rational, and that this realm is the ultimate and permanent ground and source of the religious emotions."

Keyser's gift to us at Columbia, or at least to me, was a daily reminder that the intelligent understanding of the life that is within our reach leads to richer and richer glimpses of life which is at present above us or beyond. It seemed to me then, and still more so now, that Keyser had the philosophy of a builder, a poet, a creator. He kindled something in all who listened to him.

3

When Columbia College moved up to Morningside Heights in 1896, a red brick building once fairly handsome stood at the northeast corner of Broadway and 116th Street. Here during my undergraduate days the University housed its Superintendent of Buildings and Grounds. In my senior year the structure had reached such a condition of decay that it was abandoned as a residence, and the rooms on the ground floor were occupied by MacDowell's classes in music. I have a particularly vivid memory of the largest room on the south side of the building, in which he permitted me to rehearse the chorus of *The Governor's Vrouw*. By 1909, when I returned from Amherst, the building, still further advanced on the road to ruin, became the Faculty Club. Here we lunched and on occasion dined, and here Dean Keppel, in the not uncomfortable lounge on the second floor, held faculty smokers for preliminary discussion of prickly questions. In 1923 the faculty transferred their eating and other non-intellectual activities to the new club house at Morningside Drive and 117th Street. The old building was torn down to make way for the School of Business, and some magnificent old trees disappeared with it.

The new Faculty Club was in many ways an enrichment of a teacher's life at Columbia, but I reserve a special gratitude for conversations at the crowded lunch tables of the old house. I usually ate there at noon, sometimes with other members of the English department, more often with a brilliant group whose thoughtfulness and wit attracted all the younger teachers, no matter to what department they belonged.

Easily first in the circle was James Harvey Robinson, then at the height of his remarkable powers. Near him we were likely to find James Thomson Shotwell, Charles Austin Beard, Vladimir Gregorievitch Simkhovitch, and on days of special good fortune, Michael Idvorsky Pupin.

With Professor Robinson I had taken no undergraduate courses. In those days he specialized in the history of the Renaissance, and when my graduate work directed my attention to the English Renaissance, I regretted a lost opportunity. As far as possible I made up for it by slipping into his classroom from time to time, by reading everything he wrote, and by missing none of his public lectures—which were altogether too few. His famous wit did not yet distinguish his discourses. His lectures stimulated by the range and weight of scholarship rather than by felicity of word or phrase.

When I left the Graduate School he was closing a chapter in his personal development and was about to find himself in the later philosophy for which he is best remembered. His early phase was distinguished by conscientious and tireless research. I imagine that his best students then learned from him to hunt down all material to its source and to have no patience with guess-work. The habit of skeptical questioning led Robinson far.

In the concluding weeks of graduate residence I heard him give a talk before his colleagues of the History department. The meeting was held in a classroom in an upper floor of the Low Library. Professor William Milligan Sloane presided with a ponderous courtesy which matched his portly figure. Professor Robinson by contrast, was slender in appearance and keenly intellectual.

He spoke on his favorite subject, the Renaissance, but not from any angle his colleagues may have expected. In a grave and even tone he informed them that the Renaissance was not, as he had once supposed and had long taught, a period of history, but rather an area of ignorance and uncertainty. He was now convinced that no honest historian could say when the Renaissance began or when it ended. The truth, perhaps, was that the Renaissance never had begun, and would never end.

Robinson's colleagues seemed surprised, or even disturbed, but most of his hearers took his statements in silence. Only Professor Sloane harried him with the question whether the period in which Henry VIII and Francis I had their careers would not remain essentially the same even if Professor Robinson preferred not to call it the Renaissance, or even if he insisted that the period be called by no name at all. Robinson, with his slow, reluctant smile, suggested that Professor Sloane had missed the point. Perhaps so, but I thought Sloane's question made sense.

This incident seemed far in the past when I began to seek Professor Robinson day after day in the old Faculty Club. He had reached his modern phase. He was warm and kindly unless you insisted on being dull or stupid, in which case he would rouse himself to deal with you as you deserved.

He was always possessed by a warm and kindly love of human beings; however, he seemed at times to cover his emotions with protective thought. But as he grew older he acquired an impish playfulness which enriched without contradicting whatever was intellectual and distinguished in his character. He remained as I had first known him, a learned man, but now he could put his scholarship at a moment's notice, to very simple uses.

I became extremely fond of him, perhaps because he teased me for my youth and for what he called my romantic optimism. More than once he teased me in public, or even crossed swords in print, when a gay mood possessed him.

In April, 1916, Doctor Abraham Flexner, writing in the *Review of Reviews,* suggested that a proper education would teach children only what they need for their immediate tasks in life. More remote or cultural subjects should be postponed or omitted. A few days later, on April 15, I addressed the following lines to Dr. Flexner, in the editorial page of the *New York Evening Post.*

Ode to Doctor A—— F——

Just after the Board had brought the school up to date,
To prepare you for your Life Work
Without teaching one superfluous thing,
Jim Reilly presented himself to be educated.
He wanted to be a bricklayer.

So they taught him to be a perfect bricklayer
And nothing more.
He knew so much about bricklaying that the
    contractor made him a foreman.
But he knew nothing about being a foreman.
So he spoke to the School Board about it,
And they put in a night course for him
On how to be a foreman
And nothing more.
He became so excellent a foreman that the
    contractor made him a partner.
But he knew nothing about figuring costs,
Nor about bookkeeping,
Nor about real estate,
And he was too proud to go back to night school.
So he hired a tutor, who taught him these things.

> Prospering at last, and meeting other men
>   as wealthy as he,
> Whenever the conversation started, he'd say to himself:
> "I'll lie low till it comes my way—
> Then I'll show 'em!"
> But they never mentioned bricklaying,
> Nor the art of being a foreman,
> Nor the whole duty of being a contractor,
> Nor figuring costs,
> Nor real estate;
> So Jim never said anything.
> But he sent his son to college.

That last line was an error. At lunch the next day Robinson and the usual group were laughing over an early edition of the *Evening Post*. They overdid their applause and congratulations; I knew I was in for something. On April 17 the *Evening Post* carried Robinson's reply.

Ode to Professor J—— E——

Jim Reilly's son Tom didn't know what he
    wanted to do,

So he took Latin and Mathematics and hoped
  they'd discipline his mind,
And prepare him for sharing in polite intercourse.
After three years he knew that two straight lines
  perpendicular to the same plane
Are parallel to each other.
And for a short time he could say what were
  both *sine* and *cosecant;*
But a month after the examination he unhappily
  forgot which was which.
He had learned a list of diminutives; only
  culum and *bulum* remained to him—
So sweet was their euphony.
He knew the mute with "l" or "r" played a
  mystic role in the higher life,
Which in moments of depression he felt he didn't
  grasp.
An old book by an old man for the old
Tightened the reins of his youthful spirit.
When he reached the two gates of slumber at
  the end of Lib. VI
They gave him ready exit, and he never
  began Lib. VII
But he had the elements of a liberal education, and,
Like his philistine father before him,
Whenever the conversation started he'd say
  to himself:
"I'll lie low till it comes my way—
Then I'll show 'em."
But they never mentioned the caesural pause,
And rarely the first Archilochian strophe,
Nor Vercingetorix, nor the mute with "l" or "r."
He had never got far enough to meet a
  reflection of Horace's
About those on whose cradles
  Melpomene smiles,
But he knew he couldn't play an
  Isthmian game as well as T.R.
Father Jim took him into the office.

He did not seem the worse for disci-
plining his mind,
He could make a deal *unice securus,*
However disadvantageous to the buyer,
And knew the difference betwixt a
Martini and a Bronx,
And appreciated the roundness of a
maiden's arm,
Without the help of Horace.

4

James Shotwell and Charles Beard were close friends, both of them, of course, warm admirers of Robinson. It was my good fortune when I first returned from Amherst to serve on the Administration Committee of the College with Shotwell, and to learn the soundness of his scholarship and his preoccupation with large problems. Even then, before war broke, he was convinced it was coming, also that peace would not be restored until the nations learned to arbitrate their differences. After the war he was in Paris with Professor Charles Haskins and the other historians whom President Wilson took along to guide him, whether or not he availed himself of their advice. To this day Shotwell has continued active in all movements toward international cooperation. I think him modest and tireless, servant of humanity, as among the noblest spirits of our time.

He could not be so well known nor could he exert the same kind of influence as Robinson, since he had none of Robinson's brilliance or wit. Of Canadian birth and training, he was as British in his temperament as Robinson was American. His qualities were solid rather than dazzling. As a teacher of history he is remembered at Columbia for his earnestness, his thoroughness, his patience. At the Faculty Club tables I have seen him smile, especially when James Robinson or Vladimir Simkhovitch were setting off their fireworks, but it is not his smile, however kind, that I remember best.

Charles Beard combined in a fantastic way Shotwell's seriousness of manner with Robinson's extraordinary powers of expression. There was no one at Columbia in the second decade of this century who could rival Beard as an orator. Others excelled him in wit and in the subtleties of civilized conversation, but he had no match in that type of political eloquence which democracy engenders. More than once I heard him address the student body on some question about which I disagreed with him, but while he spoke I could feel persuasion creeping over me, as it crept over the boys. He had a fine voice, but what carried conviction was his own utter belief, at least for the moment, in what he was saying. An avowed Socialist, he fancied himself the object of much criticism among the University authorities. No doubt any conservative would keep his eye on him, since socialism was dreaded then as communism is now, and he spoke and wrote with such fervor that he must have been regarded as a threat. Anyone who has scholarship and clear ideas, warm emotions, deep convictions, and the gift to sway his hearers, is potentially dangerous.

In more recent years Beard is known chiefly, I suppose, for his fine books on American history. In 1911 and 1912 he was admired by Columbia undergraduates as a great teacher who gave to many of them a new understanding of the American political system and of the organization of American government, both Federal and State. So far as I can recall he made no contribution, as Robinson did, to the broad development of human intelligence, nor did he show any of Shotwell's concern over international relations. He seemed to me a simple and genuine American patriot, perhaps a potential isolationist.

5

Vladimir Simkhovitch, Professor of Economic History, was one of the most stimulating talkers I have known, a daring wit when he was in the mood, sometimes recklessly brilliant in his sallies, but never needing to go outside his own professional subject for material for his fun-making and his satire.

He was born to wealth in a conservative Russian family where he shocked his elders by his leaning toward liberal ideas. The old Czarist government feared him before he was out of school, and disciplined him as soon as he reached the university and joined a revolutionary group. Since his scholarly abilities developed quite as fast as his revolutionary propensities, he was not seriously inconvenienced when the government exiled him. Moving over into Germany he took the degree of Ph.D. at the University of Halle in 1898. For one year his father continued Vladimir's rather handsome allowance.

But when he married Mary Melinda Kingsbury the confused old gentleman cut him off without a cent, apparently under the impression that American women were not to be distinguished from grass-skirted South Sea Islanders.

Vladimir brought his wife at once to New York, and secured a modest post as buyer and custodian of rare books in the Columbia University Library. For this work he had equipped himself in days of affluence by making a private collection of manuscripts, ikons, and other works of art. He has always been an expert in several fields not directly connected with economic history.

I first met him in the University Library. No one could use that building without having frequent occasion to notice his slender alert figure, his thick black hair, his large dark eyes, and his aptitude for conversation. I had no talk with him at that period, I being a mere student accumulating credits for the doctorate in a subject not likely to appeal to an economic historian. But if Vladimir wasn't talking to me when I first saw him, he was talking to someone else. The other man was listening.

Every autumn the academic year began for me when Vladimir showed up at the lunch table and unloosed his gay nonsense. "Any good students this year?" we would ask. He would knit his brow, pretending to be serious.

"My seminar is very promising. I have six industrious young men, and one beautiful young woman. This morning I dismissed the six, who do not need me. I shall devote myself to the beautiful young woman."

If I remember Vladimir for his gay talk it is because he added much to Columbia life by his high spirits, his zest for life, and his unusual social gift, for his interest in serious subjects was wide, deep, and apparently inexhaustible. Mrs. Simkhovitch's settlement work at Greenwich House had his quick sympathy and no doubt his practical aid—though whenever I have spent an hour in his home the talk was of Greek or Chinese art. In many discussions of Russia today Vladimir comes to mind illustrating characteristics from the old Russia which I persist in looking for in the new, characteristics both intellectual and emotional, a blend of scientific curiosity and esthetic insight.

6

Michael Pupin, physicist and inventor, resembled Professor Keyser in the simple, direct quality of his thought. I suppose they both were in essence mathematicians. Pupin also resembled Simkhovitch in the originality of his ideas and in his unconventional ways of expressing them. He seemed as native to the University campus as the old trees that survived among the formal buildings. But no professor could be less academic. His unusual life is recorded in his book, *From Immigrant to Inventor,* the most striking passages of which he sometimes retold at the faculty lunch table. As a boy he spent his nights on the Serbian plains watching cattle, studying the stars, or making elementary experiments in the transmission of sound through the earth. He and his fellow herdsmen would stick their knives in the ground, and telegraph to each other by tapping on the wooden handles.

His temperament must have been poetic as well as scientific; certainly, science as he talked of it seemed identical with poetry. The boyhood nights spent under stars planted thoughts in him which led not only to his inventions in long-distance communication but to speculations far beyond.

According to his own account he came to America with five cents in his pocket, and with no other possessions except the suit on his back and the red fez on his head. His enterprise and energy so impressed the immigration authorities at Castle Garden that they let him in on his promise to get a job immediately. Five years from the date of his landing he passed the entrance examinations to Columbia College with high marks that won him a scholarship. He was a champion wrestler, but he had the admiration of his classmates chiefly for his intellectual achievements and for his winning personality. In his junior year he was elected President of his class. He was graduated in 1883 with honors in Greek, mathematics and science, and in the same week he received his final papers as an American citizen. It was said of him later that if his confidence in the United States as a land of opportunity was excessive, the reason was that he assumed in every youthful immigrant talents and character as remarkable as his own. To him all doors opened.

I remember him standing one January afternoon in the pulpit of the University Chapel, delivering the annual commemoration address in honor of the University dead. As usual, he spoke in a tone of happy seriousness, apparently unaware that his hearers were startled as well as fascinated. His dark features and his massive figure, in colorful gown and hood, rose high above us. His first words were these, approximately:

"This week, one of my students came into my office. She is extremely good-looking.

" 'Professor Pupin,' she said, 'I hear you will preach in chapel next Sunday.'

" 'That is true,' said I.

" 'But upon what subject?'

" 'God. Is there any other subject?'

"She laughed. 'Professor Pupin, you are a scientist. You do not believe in God.'

" 'Not believe? I get messages from God every day.'

" 'You do? Tell me what was the most recent message?'

" 'It came only a minute ago. I learned it is possible for beauty to exist in a vacuum.'

" 'Well, Professor Pupin, half of that message I can accept, the other half I reject.'

" 'Young woman,' I said, 'when the message comes from God, you accept all of it or nothing.' "

Few universities could hope to number among its professors so great a scientist as Pupin, so inspiring a teacher, so beloved a companion, so admirable a citizen. At Columbia he taught us by example how to make the best of life. He found his opportunity in this country, chiefly in New York, and as student and mature scientist chiefly on the Columbia campus. But even if he had remained in Serbia, that mind of' his and that insatiable spirit would have found his proper destiny.

CHAPTER VIII

Teachers and Educators
Ruffled by War

1

DURING my six Amherst years Columbia had grown, but also had suffered many losses. Woodberry and MacDowell were gone, George Rice Carpenter was dead. Many of my former teachers were still active, and some disclosed new abilities, of which they themselves had not perhaps been aware. Professor James C. Egbert, sound scholar but unexciting teacher with whom I had once endured a course of Livy, now as director of the new Extension department was organizing with social imagination and considerable freedom from academic red tape, classes for adults in all subjects, scheduled in the late afternoon or in the evening, for the benefit of workers who wished to study while earning their living. Popular education of the modern kind was introduced to Columbia by Dr. Egbert. Because he was fond of music and a personal admirer of Walter Henry Hall, expert trainer of choirs and choral groups, he brought Dr. Hall to the University Chapel, supported him in a program of winter and summer concerts, both choral and orchestral—thus inaugurating the permanent revival of the Music department.

Professor Clarence Hoffman Young still taught Greek archaeology, and Professor Nelson Glenn McCrea still taught the philosophy of Latin poets, very much as they had done when I was a freshman and a sophomore. Edward Delavan Perry, who combined scholarship with grace and wit, now delighted many a faculty gathering with his amusing and often beautiful verses. In his classroom, listening to him take Greek tragedy to pieces, I had never suspected his humane gifts.

In the English department William P. Trent, my old friend, remained, a survival with Brander Matthews from the department which Price and Carpenter had built up. Carpenter was now succeeded as secretary of the English department by Ashley Horace Thorndike, who came to Columbia from Wesleyan University. Charles Sears Baldwin, pupil of Professor Price, was brought from Yale University to teach in Barnard College and the Graduate School, "Shakespeare" Baldwin, for his resemblance to the Bard.

In many ways he was unique among the English teachers whom I have known. For one thing he really taught the science of rhetoric, leaning rather to the old-fashioned school of Professor Genung at Amherst than to the modern methods of George Carpenter. Yet Baldwin himself was a charming writer, and he soon proved in his Barnard classes that he could teach others to write well.

Perhaps his success in getting up-to-date results from what seemed to me somewhat outmoded methods can be explained by the fact that he was a sincere medievalist, not simply an admirer of Gothic architecture and the legends of King Arthur and his knights, but in every department of his thinking he was more at ease with the ideals of the Middle Ages than with our own time. Profoundly religious, he preferred medieval expressions of religion. I think he would have liked a monastic life of prayer, meditation, study, and teaching. He was a charming gentleman, or better, he was a saint. The sweetness and unselfishness of his character was all the more lovable because of his strong sense of humor.

In the three years before our entry into the First World War there was a mild but very real outbreak of religious interest on the Columbia campus. The influence of Professor Baldwin had something to do with it, also the visit to the University of the Reverend Harvey Officer, of the Order of the Holy Cross. It may be that Baldwin inspired Father Officer's preaching mission, which lasted a week or so and attracted large gatherings in the University Chapel. At the moment we did not comment on the contrast between the appeal of Father Officer's talks and the popularity of James Harvey Robinson's courses. For a season the philosophy of faith and the philosophy of skepticism had a hearing, as it were, side by side.

Ashley Thorndike was no medievalist, and the temporary wave of mysticism touched him as little as it did Brander Matthews or Trent or my old teachers and life-long friends, William Tenney Brewster and George Clinton Densmore Odell. Brewster taught and occupied administrative posts at Barnard. Odell taught in Columbia College and increasingly in the Graduate School. He was then on the verge of undertaking his monumental history of the New York stage.

Ashley Thorndike, like his famous brothers, Edward Lee the psychologist, and Lynn the historian, was an attractive and powerful character, in certain important respects quite different from George Rice Carpenter. Carpenter had been a good executive. He had planned for the English department with imagination and wise judgment of character, and in personal contacts with colleagues and students he was gentle and affectionate.

Ashley Thorndike was gentle too in his way, very human and sympathetic, almost fatherly in his watchfulness over his students in the Graduate department. He was a sound scholar, a literary historian rather than a critic. He wrote competently as a scholar must, but he was no writer in the sense that Woodberry was, or even Brander Matthews. Professional writing he called journalism, using the term perhaps playfully, but never as a compliment. When I wrote *The Private Life of Helen of Troy* he remarked to a colleague that he had always feared I was at heart a journalist rather than a scholar.

His talent was for organization and administration. He ran the

English department well, as he would have run well a small college. When I say he "ran" the English department I mean a compliment, but also I would imply a certain domineering or dictatorial tendency. I can illustrate by an episode which takes one more liberty with the chronological order of events.

In 1924 when Brander Matthews resigned I wanted the department to call Stuart Sherman from Illinois. Thorndike did not want him. I wanted Stuart because he was a writer, a distinguished practitioner of the art he taught. That was the very reason Thorndike wouldn't have him.

I told President Butler my reasons for wanting Stuart in the department, and Butler, who had made his acquaintance at meetings of the National Academy and who admired his writings, agreed enthusiastically. I spoke also to Professor Trent, who liked the idea. Stuart had been associated with us in the *Cambridge History of American Literature*. Having gone so far I let the matter rest for a while, expecting Trent and the President to discuss it sooner or later with Thorndike.

One morning on the way to my office in Hamilton Hall I stopped at the University Clinic to let Dr. Harold B. Keyes take a look at a handsome carbuncle on my neck. He promptly made a deep incision in me and swathed my neck in bandages. A few minutes later my office telephone rang. Thorndike's voice sounded with something less than its usual friendliness—in fact, in a tone of sharp command.

"John, will you come over to my office at once?"

I was pleased to think of the shock my bandaged neck would create. When I walked into Thorndike's office the effect was dramatic. Perhaps we had better postpone our interview since it had to do with a disagreement between us, and he didn't wish to add to my discomforts. I told him I was quite comfortable in spite of appearances, and would rather get at our discussion immediately.

He then said courteously but firmly that from various sources he had learned of my conversation with the President about Stuart

Sherman. The impression had been created on the campus that Stuart was to be called. It was therefore important that I be told, what I ought to have known anyway, that I had no right to speak directly to the President on any subject which concerned the department. All communications to the President on departmental business must be transmitted through the executive officer, who happened to be not John Erskine but Ashley Thorndike. Ashley Thorndike had no intention, in conclusion, of adding Stuart Sherman to the Columbia English department. But for the moment the important thing for me to grasp was the fact that I was a private individual, and must accept the discipline of the department.

This pretty stiff doctrine was announced at length and with force. I replied in kind, and for a moment we whaled away at each other. I told Thorndike I could not accept his theory that the policy of the department was exclusively in his hands. The departmental regulations named him merely as our secretary. I thought that eventually the choice of Brander's successor ought to be discussed openly by the whole department. I would then abide cheerfully by the majority decision.

As to discussing departmental affairs or not discussing them with President Butler, I reminded Thorndike that I had known Butler since college days and had the impression that he welcomed discussions of anything that concerned the good of the University. So long as he would listen to me, I would tell him anything that was on my mind. Since Thorndike seemed to forbid any such communication, I begged to protest that the department was not a labor union, and that its secretary should not assume the authority or the manner of a labor leader. Thorndike flashed back that the department *was* essentially a union, and that it could tolerate only loyal members. After that we both felt, perhaps, that we had reached a dead end.

But Thorndike was angrier at me than I supposed, and for once his good sense failed him. He called a meeting of the full professors in the department, told them of our conversation, and asked for a vote of confidence. He wished the vote to approve three propositions which he would report to the President and the Trustees. The propositions were: 1) It is unnecessary to add to our English department anybody from outside. 2) In particular it is undesirable to call Stuart Sherman. 3) Vacancies should be filled by promoting younger teachers. Note: From these propositions Professor Erskine dissents.

He read this rigmarole with a slight tremble in his voice. Professor Trent immediately protested against the gratuitous insult to Sherman. If no one was to be called from outside, Sherman's name need not be mentioned.

Thorndike accepted the change. The motions now stood: No one should be called from the outside; vacancies should be filled by promotion; and John Erskine dissented.

I had been thinking as fast as I could. "Thorndike, I agree that the young men should be promoted, if they are competent. But I can't believe there is no one in any other university whose coming would add strength to us."

Thorndike again accepted the amendment, and with such good humor that I thought the storm had blown over, and that when he reached his office he would throw his resolutions into the waste-basket. But late that afternoon Fred Coykendall, of the Trustees, stopped for a moment at my Hamilton Hall office to ask the meaning of the resolutions from Thorndike which President Butler had just read to the Board. Fred said his fellow Trustees had noted my modest admission that there might be other good scholars and teachers somewhere in the world. Was I the only member of the department who thought so?

So Stuart Sherman did not come to Columbia. He did come to New York, however, as editor of the *Herald Tribune* literary supplement. Thorndike gave a dinner in his honor at the Faculty Club. Afterward Stuart reported that Thorndike during the evening expressed in very handsome terms his regret that there had not been an opening for him in the Columbia English department.

2

I resume my memories now in their chronological order.

Returning from Amherst in 1909, I found in the department of Comparative Literature Woodberry's pupil and former assistant, Joel Elias Spingarn, still teaching, having just been promoted to a professorship. The new head of the department, Jefferson Butler Fletcher, I had not met before, though he was well known among literary scholars. A graduate of Harvard College in 1887, he had been an instructor in English at Cambridge from 1890 to 1902. For the next two years he had been Assistant Professor of Comparative Literature at Harvard, and in 1904 he had been brought to Columbia as Professor of Comparative Literature to replace Woodberry.

I have always supposed that though he was a Harvard man, he was more sympathetic with Spingarn than with my old teacher. Shortly before his resignation from Columbia, Woodberry had started *The Journal of Comparative Literature,* a scholarly magazine edited by himself with the collaboration of Fletcher and Spingarn, both of whom were specialists in the literature of the Italian Renaissance, as Woodberry was not. He had, however, a wider range of literary sympathy than either. It may have been that Spingarn, when Woodberry left Columbia, suggested Fletcher to succeed him.

Spingarn was profoundly interested in social causes, and active always on behalf of the underprivileged and the oppressed. His name is permanently associated with the awards he established for the recognition and encouragement of talent in the Negro race. He was not only a scholar, he had courage, both physical and moral. Fletcher too had courage. Through the four years of the First World War he made a heroic record at the front, in the ambulance service first of the French Army, then of the American. Spingarn went to France as an officer in a Negro regiment.

Here were two men of the old Renaissance pattern, scholars who responded to the calls of citizenship, whether in peace or in war. One might have thought that neither would ever be involved directly or indirectly in campus quarrels of professors. But in 1909 animosities were fermenting at Columbia in the literary departments. The Brander Matthews-Woodberry feud had not burned itself out. Some teachers of literature trained in dry-as-dust methods were concerned over the growing popularity of ideas which Woodberry had stood for. The division of literary instruction at Columbia between the English department and the department of Comparative Literature had never commended itself to the English department. Perhaps Woodberry's resignation raised a hope that the work in Comparative Literature might be swallowed up and amalgamated again with the English program.

I am describing what was in 1909 a vague, almost an atmospheric, condition. It could not be ignored, but I had not been on the Columbia teaching staff long enough to know what all my colleagues were thinking. I had no part in the row when it came. My opinions of the issues now are based on information gathered later, and on later experiences.

I believe that the study of literature must be the study of more than one literature. The old-fashioned English department now seems out of date. To fill all the hours at his disposal the conventional English teacher must talk about many insignificant authors. If world literature as a whole were taught, English authors would always have a large share of attention, since England has a great literature, but insignificant writers would be omitted, to make room for Cervantes or Montaigne or Dante or Goethe—writers now studied in language courses or in the department of Comparative Literature.

Ashley Thorndike had known Professor Fletcher at Harvard and the two men were in essential agreement. Fletcher had spent most of his teaching years as an instructor in the Harvard English department. Though his own command of languages and foreign literatures was large, I doubt if he more than Thorndike felt that such culture was necessary or particularly desirable for undergraduates. Though himself a cosmopolitan he had small sympathy, I believe, with the modern ideas which underlie the contemporary hope for one united world.

Spingarn, on the other hand, was of a temperament and a racial background which Thorndike could not understand. Furthermore, Spingarn was brilliant and Thorndike was solid. Spingarn could speak foreign languages; Thorndike could read them—when it was absolutely necessary for research purposes. At no point, neither in special equipment nor in educational theory, did the two men meet. Looking back now at the inevitable collision between them, I sympathize chiefly with Spingarn, but justice to Thorndike compels me to add that Spingarn himself hastened the crash. He precipitated it partly by his attitude to his teaching obligations, and partly by the position he took in the mess over Harry Thurston Peck. In both cases, I believe, his conduct should be explained by the nervous breakdown which eventually affected his mind and brought his life to an early close.

He denied that he neglected his students, but said he found it impossible to conform to meaningless academic routine. What routine he had in mind, I do not know. So far as I observed, his duties were limited to giving the courses which he himself chose to give, and to guiding the work of the students whom he himself permitted to take a Doctor's degree under him.

One afternoon, when I happened to be in his office, a student knocked. We could see the outline of his figure through the ground glass of the door, and Spingarn gave a half-humorous exclamation of embarrassment.

"He has come to hear my opinion of his thesis. I haven't yet read it. I forgot he had an appointment today."

When the student knocked again, Spingarn opened the door, greeted the boy with an austerity which implied a rebuke, and told him to come the following week at a more convenient time.

Later in the spring the English and Comparative Literature departments scheduled the examinations for their Ph.D. candidates. Since there were many candidates, the examinations had to be put at available hours all six days of the week, including Saturday morning. Spingarn wrote to Thorndike asking that the examinations for candidates who had written their theses under him should be set not later than Friday afternoon, since he wished to spend his Saturdays in the country. Though the request occasioned sarcastic remarks from professors who also would have been glad to be free on Saturdays, we fixed Spingarn's examinations not later than Friday afternoon.

On Friday I lunched with him at the old Faculty Club, and particularly enjoyed his remarkable talk. He seemed in the best of spirits. When we started afterward toward Fayerweather Hall, he turned abruptly toward 116th Street.

"Where are you going?"

"I'm taking a train."

"But your examination begins in a minute!"

"I shall not attend it."

The examination went off badly. Most of the examiners were out of temper with the absent Spingarn. Spingarn's pupil was doubly nervous, finding himself deserted. At the conclusion some of the examiners wished to reject the candidate, or to ask him to come up for further examination when Spingarn should be present. But Professor Trent, always kind-hearted, put his foot down.

"Spingarn has been very unjust to his pupil," he told us. "We have not been in good humor. The boy has not had a fair chance. Most of us have had him in our classes; he is a good student. He must have his degree."

So the candidate was made a Doctor of Philosophy.

3

Shortly before 1909 the Columbia faculty circles were disturbed and, if truth must be told, entertained by rumors about Harry

Thurston Peck and a favorite pupil of his, the good-looking young woman whom in 1903 I had interrupted in the study of a Latin text with him.[1] The *Dictionary of American Biography* says that by 1905 he "began to show signs of mental deterioration and aberration." Odd that so many fine minds at Columbia went to pieces in the decade before the First World War! In 1908 Mrs. Peck obtained a divorce from her husband; in 1909 he married his promising pupil; in 1910 a former stenographer sued him for breach of promise.

We should remind ourselves that Professor Peck was a remarkable scholar, author of many important works, notably *Harper's Dictionary of Classical Literature and Antiquities*. With Daniel Coit Gilman and Frank Moore Colby he had recently edited the *New International Encyclopedia,* and launched and for several years directed *The Bookman,* one of the best literary monthlies we ever had in the United States. He and Dr. Butler had been closely associated in undergraduate days, and in the development of Columbia College into a modern university Peck was one of Dr. Butler's most helpful collaborators. In 1908, when his troubles began, his position in New York society and in the educational world was high. At the close of 1910 he had no position at all; he was a ruined man. The woman who sued for breach of promise gave to such papers as would use them a mass of letters he had written to her. The publication of this correspondence was a fantastic revelation of bad taste, bad judgment, weak character and sick brain. His second wife, the promising student, left him; he was ostracized by those who had admired him; the Columbia Trustees dismissed him from his professorship.

At this point Spingarn became Peck's champion. He argued that the University did wrong in dismissing Peck while the case was still in the courts. Most of the faculty agreed, but they also felt that Peck should have asked for leave of absence and should have stepped out of his professorial routine until the malodorous suit was settled. Un-

[1] *The Memory*, p. 69.

less the verdict exonerated him, no one, so far as I recall, thought he should return to the campus. I belonged to a large group who believed that whatever the court decided in the suit against him, his usefulness as a teacher was ended, and Columbia had seen the last of him.

To Spingarn the case seemed far more complicated. He believed that academic freedom was involved, and he seemed to broaden the usual concepts of academic freedom to include freedom of conduct as well as of speech. On one occasion he said in print that "freedom of speech and conduct do not exist at Columbia." We knew of course that he was not defending Peck's immoralities, nor could a person of his refined, even fastidious, nature see anything desirable in bad taste and vulgarity. But just what *was* he trying to defend? He invited his colleagues to make a formal protest on Peck's behalf; not understanding what he wished them to protest against, they declined. He retorted by publishing some satiric verses in which he described the Columbia faculty as containing,

> Seven hundred professors,
> But not a single man.

The seven hundred professors were not impressed; the argument continued informally between them and Spingarn, more seriously between Spingarn and the Trustees, between Spingarn and the President. In 1911 the Trustees abolished Spingarn's chair of Comparative Literature. In 1914 Harry Thurston Peck committed suicide.

This extraordinary and most unpleasant episode has been reported in many versions. I give here in outline my memory of what happened, but I cannot pretend to know all the facts, far less to understand all the motives. I could not discern in Peck's tragedy the slightest issue of academic freedom. I saw no reason for Spingarn's cavalier attitude toward his duties as a teacher. Ashley Thorndike was within the truth when he said that Spingarn was losing interest in his work, and in some cases was beginning to neglect the students. On the other hand, I know that Thorndike disliked Spingarn and was eager to get rid of him, just as later he refused to have Stuart Sherman in the department. His hostility, both to Spingarn and to Sherman, was not personal; he saw value in a more pedestrian type of scholarship than either of them could or would illustrate. He was by temperament on guard against original or creative natures.

When Spingarn was dismissed, Woodberry wrote him a letter of sympathy and of indignation, a very wonderful letter indeed in the noble ideal it expressed of scholarship among free minds—but to me a troubling letter in so far as it assumed much in the treatment of Peck and Spingarn which did not correspond with my knowledge of the facts. Woodberry had never made a statement to explain his own retirement from Columbia. In the letter to Spingarn much that had smoldered in him found expression. He seemed to lump himself, Peck, and Spingarn in one united instance of academic persecution. To me this did not make sense, but overlooking the emotional bias of Woodberry's letter, I could still admire it for the ideal of free inquiry which it expressed.

In 1933, three years after Woodberry's death, a group of his former pupils published a volume of his selected letters, with an introduction by Walter de la Mare. His pupils were invited to submit to the editorial committee all the Woodberry letters they had. Among those which Spingarn submitted was the eloquent and passionate one concerning his dismissal. The editorial committee, fearing the publication of that outburst would do Woodberry and Spingarn no good, fearing also perhaps that it would do Columbia harm, made what I consider the weak and most regrettable decision to leave it out of the book. Had it been included, Woodberry would have been completely and honestly represented in this, the only collection of his letters which has yet been published. He was not alw rs, as some of his admirers try to make him, a patient, inactive spirit. He had his heroic, even violent, moments, and in a cause which he believed just, he expressed himself passionately.

Since the letter was not to appear in the larger collection, I am glad that Spingarn included it in a little pamphlet called, *Two Letters from George Edward Woodberry to J. E. Spingarn,* privately printed at Amenia, New York, 1931.

4

In a sense the Spingarn case, like the Woodberry case, was never concluded at Columbia, and the death of Professor Peck did not assure the Trustees that from now on Columbia professors would behave themselves. Undoubtedly the approaching war produced everywhere a weird tension and a lack of balance. The spirit of pacifism which the University had encouraged until the threat of war appeared, suddenly became as abhorrent to the conservatives as the Communistic spirit is today. The Columbia Trustees seemed to fear disaster for the country, and unfortunately they also seemed to think themselves expert judges of true patriotism, with police power over all whom they suspected of having other ideas than theirs. In a curious way the memory of the Peck episode lingered in the Trustee mind as a smirch on the whole faculty.

In the early part of 1917 the Trustees published their intention of investigating the entire professorial group to make sure that no improper doctrines were promulgated at Columbia and that no bad examples were set to the students. With the rest of my colleagues I resented this bumptious insult. No doubt the Trustees were responsible ultimately for the instruction given at Columbia, but they had no right to go over the head of the President, the executive officer of the University, and it was a curious affront to give to the press their suspicions of us in matters which they had never discussed with us and about which they were abysmally uninformed.

On March 9 I wrote to William Barclay Parsons, of the Trustee Board, also of the Trinity Vestry, where I met him at regular intervals.

Dear Mr. Parsons

I am one of the large number of the faculty at Columbia who deeply regret the published intention of the Trustees to investigate our teaching, and it has seemed to me that in self-respect I ought to tell you how I feel about the matter, and it seemed to me also that it might be of some service to you to know privately how this matter affects men like myself who are not often in the storm center of things in the University. We feel that an unintentional slight has been put upon us by the Trustees in the publication of their plan. If you wished to re-organize your office or to investigate some part of it which seemed to be going amiss, I doubt very much if you would begin by discrediting your whole office to the extent of publicly announcing the projected reform. As I say, we take it for granted that the impression which the announcement makes was not intentional on the part of the Trustees, but I personally feel humiliated by the publication of that intention.

Having said that, I should like to say, also, that the vast majority of the faculty so far as I am able to judge would gladly support the Trustees in any investigation which they chose to make looking toward the improvement of Columbia University, provided, that the Trustees in making the investigation did not seem to cast suspicion upon us all in advance. I personally feel in so large an institution as Columbia it is entirely too easy for mediocrity and incompetence to creep into our organization and that mediocrity and incompetence are usually the causes of whatever difficulties we have. I sincerely hope the Trustees will call upon the faculties and the deans and upon all the other machinery already in existence to carry out in cooperation with them the investigation which apparently the Trustees have in mind. If the Trustees on the other hand intend to do this investigating themselves without the cooperation of the University machinery already in existence, men on the faculty who feel as I do will be compelled to conclude that the slight cast upon us by the newspaper publication of the Trustees' plan is then being aggravated, and that the lack of confidence implied in your announcement to the press was not unintentional but premeditated.

These times are so exciting that it is rather easy to make a mistake of judgment, and it may be that I am in some way embarrassing you by this letter; but if I may say so, I hope that you, as leader of the Trustees, will not miss the opportunity of enlisting the cooperation of the faculties to the utmost, and I can assure you that cooperation is here for the asking.

Mr. Parsons replied on March 12th.

My dear Prof. Erskine

I received your letter on Saturday morning just as I was leaving to attend the meeting of our committee at the University, to which, as you undoubtedly know by this time, we had invited all the Deans for a conference to discuss the matter.

In the first place, I want to thank you for your very frank letter. There is nothing that I appreciate more than frankness. I always feel that frankness indicates friendship, and I assure you that I am always at your service for advice, and especially am I open for information.

I was very much surprised to learn on Saturday that the view expressed in your letter was widely held—not universally, because I have had letters diametrically opposed to yours. I think the committee made it clear to the assembled Deans that not only was there no intentional slight to the teaching staff, but no slight that in any fairness could be imagined. The Trustees always publish an account of the meetings. Had we passed any such motion and kept it secret, then I think we could have been accused of slighting the staff. The very fact that we followed our usual course seemed to me and to all of us to mean that our actions could not be adversely criticized.

In your letter you express the hope that the Trustees will call upon the Deans and upon such machinery as is in existence to assist in carrying out the investigation proposed. Naturally, we had thought of doing nothing else, as is evidenced by the fact that our very first step was to invite a conference between all the Deans and our committee. After getting the advice of the Deans our next step is going to be one along similar lines. If you are to be at the Trinity meeting tonight, perhaps I will by that time be in a position to give you details.

We recognize the position of men like you—the sincerity, the earnestness and the honesty of the great majority of the teaching staff. We do recognize, however, that there are in the teaching staff men who are bringing discredit not only upon the University, but upon the whole profession of teaching and of scholarship in general. These men are but few; unfortunately their noise is in inverse ratio to their numbers. The condition that exists at Columbia is not singular; other universities are afflicted, I know, in the same way. It is a source of regret to me that the great body of earnest scholars who form the teaching staffs of our universities have not risen to purge themselves of their own black sheep. You know better than I do that, to go no further than our own University, there are men who have both talked and in many cases, I regret to say, practiced immorality, impiety, disloyalty, and a general discredit of what the human race has found necessary for its own preservation to be the foundations of a stable society; and yet I do not recall one single instance where any faculty has come forward of its own accord to demand that men who do such things, which the majority disapprove, should be disciplined.

A few years since at Columbia there was a very flagrant case. A professor of high rank both preached and practiced immorality. Was there a word raised from the faculty? Not one. It was left for the Trustees to act, and we were compelled to dismiss from the service of the University a man who had been a college mate of some of us, a personal friend of all.

I would very much rather have the action that the Trustees have proposed come from within. The Trustees are going to give you gentlemen every opportunity to put our University right before the world and to have Columbia set an example to all other universities not only in this country, but abroad. There is an opportunity, if the existing machinery, as you call it, will only rise to it, to establish new ideals and higher ideals in education.

5

This reply shocked me almost as much as the original statement in the public press. Mr. Parsons evidently was aware that he and the other Trustees were not correct in their procedure. The Trustees were now consulting the deans—perhaps to gather the information they should have had before they made their public criticism of the faculty. I thought I detected in the letter a tone as nearly apologetic as could possibly be expected from a man of Mr. Parsons's temperament. He rarely admitted himself in error and he practically never apologized. The wild charges he made about professors who not only preached but practiced immorality, and his theory that one of a professor's duties is to police the other professors, did not sit well with me. I could not understand why the President, whose business it is to deal with the faculty, had not been mentioned, not even now that the deans were consulted. When this whole stormy prewar period was behind us, I realized that Dr. Butler was not the sort of person to engage in a man hunt, that his brand of pacifism had never elected him, even temporarily, to the lunatic fringe, and that he had not favored some of the Trustee persecutions which ended in the dismissal of professors. But at the moment I was perplexed by the apparent ignoring of the President as though he had gone out of existence. Perhaps the Trustees suspected even then that they could not control him if he made up his mind. Perhaps they had gone on what we might call "wildcat" adventures in patriotism.

The evening after I received the reply from Mr. Parsons I chanced to meet him with Dr. Manning, then still Rector of Trinity Parish. The two Trustees were most amicable and we had a frank talk, both of them quite sure that the faculty ought to reform itself, and I insisting that the wholesale charges of the Trustees were an insult to us all, and that the publication of the charges was altogether improper.

This particular row died out after a little while, but the Trustees took the bit in their teeth several times later, chiefly under the leadership of Mr. Parsons and Mr. Francis S. Bangs, our Number One hotheads. In the end they fired Henry W. L. Dana, who had been teaching only a short time in the English department. They also dismissed Professor James McKeen Cattell, the psychologist, depriving him of his pension, though he had taught at Columbia for many years. Cattell waited until the war was over, and the war madness had died out. He then sued the University, and the courts restored his pension rights. The outrageous assumption of dictatorial powers drove Charles Beard into resigning. The criticism of the Columbia Trustees which accompanied his resignation can be illustrated by the incidents I have here recalled from the stormiest years in my teaching career.

CHAPTER IX

Two Extraordinary Students

1

I FIRST met Reginald Paget in the late autumn of 1914. It was the season when in-coming freshmen ask advice about their courses. He came with far more than the usual eagerness. I still see his slender figure, his bright eyes, his fine head, his alert face. But he came in a wheel-chair. He made no reference to his condition, and for the moment I did not ask about it. Obviously his feet were useless, but his hands and his arms served him well.

He told me that before he left high school he learned shorthand, and he still could do enough copying to earn a considerable income, but that was a small matter; kind friends were providing him with the means to be comfortable and to finish his education.

His only problem was how best to spend two and a half years. What would I advise for the first year? For the second? For the final four months?

"What do you intend to do then?"

His answer was simple; he gave it with a smile. "Then I shall die."

I could not speak, but quickly he put me at ease. He suffered from a progressive paralysis. Naturally he had learned all he could about his case. He would have the use of hands and arms for another two years, approximately. He was encouraged to believe his mind would remain clear, and his speech, up to the end, but when the paralysis reached his heart, he would be dead.

How should he spend his time meanwhile? That was all he cared to talk about. We agreed about his courses, and when he wheeled himself out of my study, he left me amazed and somewhat limp.

For the next two years, and approximately four months longer, he was the most brilliant student on the campus. In my own courses his classmates worried if he did not come on time. If he arrived late, he was greeted with smiles of relief. He always placed his wheel-chair just inside the door, where he could face toward me or toward the other students, turning always toward the person who at the moment was speaking.

In every classroom there is one face more eager than the others, toward which the teacher invariably turns. I turned toward Reginald Paget. Every bright remark registered a quick response in his eyes and in his smiles. It was the same, I was told, in other classes.

No one heard from him a complaint or even a reference to his condition. He was as brave a soul as I ever met, and his whole-hearted enjoyment of life put the rest of us to shame. As I came to know him better, I wondered at the inconveniences he endured. He lived in a small apartment on Amsterdam Avenue, and a very competent nurse came in to look after him and his room when she was free during the day. She was somewhat older than he. I learned his gratitude to her.

He tried to take part in the activities of his fellow students, but in everything but writing he had to be an onlooker. He wrote some poems. One which I never forgot was called "The Pacifist." It expressed the hatred of war which is in most of us, but at the moment there was a shining warship in the Hudson River. The poet confessed that the warship seemed to him beautiful.

He admitted one disappointment in his fate—just one; other

boys could dream of children, of becoming a link between the elder and the younger generation. Sometimes he felt entirely cut off, but he did not permit such thoughts to disturb him long.

In the beginning of the final half-year he failed rapidly. During the last fortnight we missed him at class, and our sessions were thoughtful, knowing that he was dying. The end came in April, 1917, and a few days later the College Chapel was crowded with his fellow students to hear a tribute to him. Perhaps their thoughts were more than any formal valedictory, considering how terrible death is at the easiest and how doubly terrible for the young. Asking how much courage and faith they would need to imitate his magnificent poise, perhaps they wondered how much education any man would ask, beyond what he had.

At the first news of his crisis I began paying daily calls on him in his Amsterdam Avenue room. When he was dead I wondered at the triumphant peace on his noble face. His faithful nurse, weeping silently, recalled the steady courage with which he had waited for the approaching Shadow.

I learned from her afterward the most surprising part of his story. To attend properly to the needs of a boy who was really a man, proved difficult in the little room where he was surrounded by neighbors, most of them sympathetic, but some of them gossipy. To give him greater peace, and also of course to express her devotion, the nurse had married him. When he died he knew with certainty that he was a father. He died in triumphant peace. He was not the last of his line. His child was a boy.

2

I met Torao Taketomo through Professor Kuryagawa, a Japanese teacher of English who came to New York just before we entered the First World War. He was lecturing on the cultural relations of his country to the United States. Since he had been a pupil of Lafcadio Hearn,[1] he paid me a courteous call by way of thanks for *Interpretations of Literature,* the two volumes of Hearn's lectures which I edited in 1915. When he said goodbye he invited me to hear the speech he was shortly to make before a group who studied the art and literature of Asia. I went. There was a good audience. The discourse was profound—but unintelligible. I do not now recall the subject. But after the applause and other evidences of international good will, the lecturer introduced a young man named Torao Taketomo.

He was about eighteen, of medium height, slender, cheerful, good-looking without conceit, and whether he knew it or not, wickedly charming. His eyes were black, his hair blue-black, his teeth whiter than white. His smile was sincere rather than facile, and his voice gentle, though he pitched it a little high, or so it seemed to Western ears.

"Mr. Taketomo works in Brooklyn," explained Mr. Kuryagawa. "His interest, however, is in the Greek art. He will perhaps desire to study poetry with you at the Columbia University. In Japan I know his father and mother. He himself is also respectable. I recommend without exception."

So Torao took my courses and I learned something of his history. His mother had studied at an American mission, and whether or not the missionaries converted her to Christianity, she had from them a training in English so thorough that she taught the language to Torao. When I first met him he was writing poems in English for American magazines, and in 1917 he published, through Duffield and Company, *Paulonia,* a translation of seven Japanese short stories.

Since he wished to become a Greek scholar, his parents gave him some travel money and sent him to the place the missionaries came from, having received the impression that it was the source of Western knowledge. Torao found himself at the Yale Divinity School.

[1] *The Memory,* p. 239.

"Professor, in two weeks I discover their interest in Greek is not mine."

Continuing his search for the classical world, he came to New York, where he discovered in much less than two weeks that the cost of living was higher than in New Haven. Too considerate of his parents to ask for more money, he found work in Brooklyn.

"What kind of work?"

"Professor, at the Brooklyn Museum—I take care of Oriental prints."

"Then you know something about prints?"

He smiled that sincere smile of his. "Professor, they *have* the prints. I *am* the Oriental."

He was an Oriental in many respects, not least in the way he would apparently read several books at the same time. But his method, however distracting it might seem to a Westerner, was for him an aid to concentration. And his comments on his reading always startled me—especially if he had read something I had written.

One day he mentioned *The Moral Obligation to be Intelligent*. "What do you think of it?"

"Professor, I presume to wonder if you have not in one place introduced a confusion of idea?"

"Where?"

"You discuss Intelligence, but at the end you translate an old Latin prayer for Wisdom. Forgive me, Professor, Intelligence and Wisdom not the same thing at all."

"Not exactly, perhaps, but almost. If you exercise your intelligence long enough, you'll accumulate some wisdom, won't you?"

"Professor, I regret—there is no connection. You say, a rat leave a sinking ship. If ship must sink, intelligent rat know how to get off. But wise rat will not take that particular ship in first place."

After the war—the first war—he returned to Japan, and on his way across the continent he mailed a happy post card whenever the train stopped. Whatever else he had on his mind there was room for trenchant criticism of architectural styles in our Middle West. For example: "Your Emerson said, Build every man his own house. Dear Professor, from the car window I reflect, every man must have done so. Best wishes from your pupil.   TORAO"

At home at last, he married and became a teacher of English literature, and soon won a name for himself as a poet. Before Pearl Harbor I could imagine him, middle-aged but youthful in heart, surrounded by his growing family, deep in his books, or explaining America to boys who grew up to fight our children. Perhaps he would tell me that his children and ours proved themselves intelligent rather than wise. I knew he would think of the tragedy with heartache, somewhat as he wrote in a letter after the earthquake:

> In my class I was discussing Epic, about Homer, Dante, and Milton. That which had most attraction for me was the subjective motive of the epic grandeur. I saw man, a hero fighting with a dark fate of life. I saw the wrath of Achilles, the defiance of Satan, which were symbolic of the human mind struggling with the destiny of Death. The great disaster taught me how to feel in such a condition. I thought I could live (was living) in the Heroic Age.
>
> You wrote me not to imitate western civilization. But there is one thing at least which I admire and am fain to imitate if I could, and that is this Epic attitude of your heroes and thinkers. Japanese is said to be a brave people, but their mind is cultivated to the negative thought of the Buddhistic idea; no, not Buddhistic but Oriental idea, for, in certain respects, Christianity itself contains much of the same attitude of mind. Your recluses and hermits are beautiful, just as beautiful as the old Japanese lyrics and romances. But they are negative. There is nothing like Browning in our poetry. I admire the vein of Odysseus' endurance in your civilization, the manliness, and the real courage. I believe in them.

But I am still very much concerned about the future state of Japanese mind in general. A social revolution might come. The dignity, the noble cause of the higher mind, might be destroyed. I trust my mind.

I forgot to tell you that Mr. Kuryagawa, who first introduced me to you, died at his summerhouse in Kamakura. His house fell upon him. It is very sad. Mr. Kuryagawa was quite popular and successful after his return from America. He wrote on Psycho-Analysis and other such subjects with which I did not quite agree. But he became a very popular critic. His last book was *Modern Opinions on Love*.

Yours Sincerely,

TORAO TAKETOMO

For many years I did not hear from Torao, and I was surprised and delighted to receive a letter from him at the end of 1946, through the kindness of Mr. Stephen G. Cutting, just home from the Orient. Of Torao's sons, whom he dearly loved, one fell in the war in Central China. In his letter to me, Torao does not mention his tragic loss. He is still trying to live as a citizen of the heroic age.

His entire letter, the first I received from him after the war, seems to me a document of importance, as showing his character in the moment. I therefore produce it here. Perhaps I do so out of vanity. I am a teacher, and Torao is my pupil. Could I have a pupil, of whom I might be prouder? The description of the surrender of Japan, of which his letter speaks, I have no right to publish here; but I hope to aid in making it accessible to American readers. It is a noble story, and Torao Taketomo has told it well.

Here is his personal letter to me:

December 4, 1945

Nishinomiya, Hyogokin, Japan.

Dear Mr. Erskine:

My first thought after the armistice was to communicate

with you, as I knew that you are one of many Americans who are thinking of us in Japan. It was my good fortune to meet with some of your soldiers and I take liberty to ask Sergeant Cutting who is now going home to take this letter to you, hoping for the chance in which he might tell you about his visits, and the pleasant visits we had during his stay in our neighborhood.

Well, I survived the war, and I have to do something for my country and for peace of the world. My work, as you know, lies in the study of literature. I am teaching English literature in a university—lecturing, reading and working among the students. This fall, at the annual conference for the study of English literature which was held at the Kyoto Imperial University, I delivered a lecture on Rousseau's influence on the English essay. My subject was about the pedestrianism, from Hooker, Ben Jonson, John Taylor, the "water poet," Bunyan, and through the eighteenth century poets and novelists to Wordsworth, and how it crystallized a type of essay under the influence of Rousseau, especially in William Hazlitt. I lectured in English, read parallel passages from the *Confessions* and *On Going a Journey*. I am glad to say there were three Americans, two soldiers and one Catholic priest, among my audience.

I finished my translation of *La Divina Commedia* during the war. It will come out among the first books to be published after four years. It took almost the best part of my lifetime, but I do not regret. I hope that I was able to do something similar to what Longfellow did for your country.

My letter became [has become] a sort of report of a student. I cannot help being so, as you are always my teacher in my mind. I will ask Sergeant Cutting to take two of my English writings to you—one on the translation of *Tanka,* [the short Japanese poems], and the other on the present situation of Japan. The latter is not complete, and I am sorry to say, not in a good copy, the better one being taken away by friend; it was printed, however, by kindness of a young American soldier who is now on his way home.— But I think you would like to read it as an expression of what we feel in Japan at present. If you approve the attempt, and if you would kindly find a publisher for it as you did for my translation of the short stories of Japan in my student days, I wish to continue in this writing and to have it published in America.

Some days ago I was reading your letter you wrote to me soon after the great earthquake of Japan, in which you prophesied somehow the present situation of our countries. Also I recollect your words about my works, which were to be done in English and in Japanese. I am following your advice, and I hope it is not too late in my life.

One of the soldiers mentioned your recent work on Jesus, and also Professor Van Doren's book on Benjamin Franklin. I will read them as soon as I get hold of them. They gave me several volumes of Armed Services Editions of the late publications in America, and I made up my mind to study more deeply in American Literature.

Yours sincerely,

TORAO TAKETOMO.

CHAPTER X

Beau Geste

1

THE news of the Armistice, November 11, 1918, was flashed to the small and crowded liner *Lorraine,* bound from New York to Bordeaux. On board were the Tardieu Mission, accompanied by high-ranking military men, notably by Colonel Edouard Jean Réquin, who had been Chief of Staff to Foch at the first Battle of the Marne. All the French who had been in Washington were going home. The war was over.

Until the Armistice news arrived I should have said the most interesting men on the ship were Jo Davidson and his friend "Steff," Lincoln Steffens. I spent all the time I could with them. Steff was going over to report the Peace Conference, Jo to make portrait busts of peacemakers, diplomats and generals. I was on my way back to France after hurried hours in New York gathering teachers and textbooks for postwar army schools.

Colonel Réquin was a familiar type of French army officer, of medium height, trained down to muscular agility. He wore the conventional army moustache; otherwise his face was a mask. I do not remember seeing him smile. But the news of the Armistice transfigured him. Though like the other French officers he knew what the war cost in blood and suffering, with slight hope of a last-

ing peace after all, yet he adored Marshal Foch, and at the moment
he thought, and wanted to speak, only of his victorious commander.

After dinner that evening Jo, Steffens and I sat in the smoking
room till past midnight listening to stories of Foch at the Marne,
and studying the Colonel's sketch book, every page of which, except
one, had caught the Marshal in some characteristic attitude—on a
stepladder, studying a wall map—or listening with stoic calm to a
courier with bad news—or presiding over a Staff conference, or
talking with a *poilu*. Jo admired the drawings; Colonel Réquin
was an artist of quality. But the value he attached to the sketch
book was sentimental and personal; he had carried the bulky port-
folio to America with him; he was carrying it back to France. It
was his most precious possession.

We asked what the last page was reserved for. Réquin shook his
head—for something very important, he did not know what.

Next evening the ship gave a party to raise funds for the relief
of wounded sailors and soldiers. There was an auction at which Jo
Davidson presided alternately with Owen Johnson, the writer; there
was also a voting contest at five francs a vote, for the most beautiful
woman on board. The competition at first lacked focus; with the
returning French missions there were a number of ladies who deserved not to be overlooked, and the gentlemen of their acquaintance rose to the opportunity, but gradually one candidate forged
ahead, a sprightly actress who had the support of all the younger
officers. Their consolidated homage found expression in the pur-
chase of tickets in large blocks. The alluring lady was sure to win.
She had over five thousand votes.

At the door of the room, watching the fun, stood two husky
Americans, with skin which suggested an outdoor life. A rumor
circulated that they owned copper mines, but the idea may have
been based on their complexion. Through the evening they cast no
vote, but when the final ballot was called for, they glanced at each
other. Then one of them took his poker face to the front table,
bought a large handful of ballots, marked them, and stuffed them

into the box. A few minutes later we learned that Madame So-and-So was the victor, having outdistanced her nearest rival by several thousand votes.

Madame So-and-So had not previously been mentioned. After an astonished silence the mysterious winner was invited to stand up and acknowledge our applause. In a far corner beside a wounded French veteran—he had lost an arm—a sweet-faced little woman stopped knitting and rose to make a bashful bow. She had accompanied her husband on a mission to America, and now on the return voyage chance had placed them at the same dining table with the two Westerners, who came to feel that she and her man were the finest people on the boat.

The applause was terrific. When he could make himself heard Colonel Réquin rose to accept what for him was a challenge. If Madame the Winner would meet him in the lounge next morning, he would draw her portrait in the one remaining page of his Foch album.

Of course we were all in the lounge on the hour, all who could squeeze in. The portrait was finished. After Madame, tearful with pleasure, had expressed her approval of it, the Colonel passed it around for us all to have a look. When it came back at last, he offered it to her again. Her face brightened. "I did want to see it once more!"

Then with a happy sigh she gave it up, but he refused to take it. "It is yours, Madame."

She gasped. "But Marshal Foch, Colonel! It is your memory of him!"

He lighted a cigarette. "Madame, it is your portrait."

Then he went out for a stroll on the deck.

2

I have told elsewhere [1] how I happened to be in France from the beginning of 1918, and to what services I was assigned, first at

Haudainville and Sommedieue, with the Second French Army, afterward in educational work with the American troops.

My hurried trip home just before the Armistice was for the purpose of gathering textbooks and recruiting teachers for the educational work the Army planned after the war. Officers and men would have opportunities to study in British and French schools and universities. More elementary instruction would be offered throughout the Army, wherever the troops came to rest when the fighting stopped. And though we did not foresee this part of our future, we were now on the way to set up the American Army University at Beaune, in Burgundy. No other educational experience ever did more for me than this Beaune episode. All who took part in it seemed to surpass themselves in devotion and tact, as though the recollection of Colonel Réquin's *beau geste* set the tone of our behavior.

The University at Beaune was improvised to care for students who could not be accommodated in the British and French institutions though our Allies made generous sacrifices to receive as many American students as possible. At the close of the Second World War our G.I.'s crowded back into our schools, impatient to recover what they had lost in the years of fighting. After the first war British and French boys were just as eager to get on with their interrupted studies. For them that particular war had been long; for us it was short. But they put themselves to one concluding inconvenience to make room for students from our Army. Though we had not been long in the war, they knew we had crossed the ocean to get in it at all, and our wish to study at their universities was, they felt, a compliment they must accept.

No doubt the willingness to make room for as many Americans as possible looked prudently toward the future. They knew our unwillingness to get into a European war, and they feared our eagerness to go home and stay there. They would do all they could to bind us to them by at least a few memories of Europe at peace,

[1] *The Memory*, pp. 256-60.

and by cultural ties. Yet it was still a sacrifice to make room for so many of us just then. When we realized that some of us, at best, would be left out, we decided that the Army must set up its own university. When I say that "we" decided, I mean General Robert I. Rees and the Army Educational Commission, of which I was chairman. The other Commissioners were Frank Ellsworth Spaulding, then Superintendent of Schools in Cleveland, Ohio, later Chairman of the department of Education in the Yale Graduate School; and Kenyon Leech Butterfield, President of the Massachusetts Agricultural College. In the work of the Commission Dr. Butterfield looked after instruction in agriculture and in the trades; Dr. Spaulding organized instruction of high school and common school quality, and I was responsible for the universities and professional schools.

If we all had taken an attitude less chivalrous than Colonel Réquin's the Commission would have been hopelessly at odds over the proposal to set up an Army University at Beaune. Both Spaulding and Butterfield were against it. They believed the three Commissioners should function as a unit, advising each other, and constantly assisting all parts of the Army. If I set up a big school at Beaune, I should have to stay in that place, and there would be no prospect of educational jaunts together. To be sure, the Army was receiving daily far more applications for university study than could be granted without the creation of another university, but it would be impossible, they argued, to organize in so short a time a school of any quality.

My view was—and General Rees agreed—that we could not turn down the applications for instruction without at least trying to satisfy them. The Commission need not be separated, though we certainly would be stationary. Dr. Butterfield would have his agricultural laboratory near Beaune, at Allerey, where the Army leased a farm. He and Spaulding could have their quarters at Beaune, where we could confer daily, and from that central point they could direct their work in the field.

Perhaps they were convinced by results. In any case they were good sports, and aside from this one big question, we saw eye to eye.

No, I must modify that statement. Dr. Butterfield was a good deal of a pacifist, and he feared the influence of the military mind upon education. Just why he joined the Army Educational Commission I can't guess. We were working for the Fifth or Training Section of the General Staff, under the command of professional soldiers. I fear that Dr. Butterfield considered the military authority an intrusion upon his dreams of a peaceful world, which should be convinced of the importance of agriculture.

When the University at Beaune was established I had been a teacher for about fifteen years, first in a small college, then in a large university. I had not grasped the possibilities of educational error and disaster in both places. There was not yet a presidential crisis at Amherst, and what now appears to be the literary decline of the English department had not yet been inaugurated at Columbia. I could still believe that civilian educators could produce a better kind of school than army officers, and that the humanities would fare best when far removed from military discipline.

Beaune converted me. I gladly confess now that General Rees and Colonel Ira Louis Reeves, the Superintendent, later the military President of the Army University, set an example of justice and good sense which academic administrators might imitate.

I learned from the Army the main principles of administration— to keep rules and regulations few and clear—never to let lines of authority get crossed—always to communicate through channels.

The civilian-military organization of the A.E.F. University was announced by Colonel Reeves in a General Order, the day after it had been formulated by the Colonel and the University Council in an informal discussion. If the regulations seem to place final authority in the Colonel himself, as Superintendent of the University, it should be remembered that the University was set up by an army in the field, which in spite of the Armistice might have to fight again.

HEADQUARTERS

American A.E.F. University

A.P.O. 909

General Order

No. 6.   23 February, 1919.

1. The following plan of administration of the educational organization of the University has been approved, and is published for the information and guidance of all concerned.

Educational Organization of the University

1. The University will be administered by military authority through the Superintendent of the University, with the advice of the Army Educational Commission and its experts on educational matters as defined in G.O. Nos. 9 and 30, c.s., G.H.Q., A.E.F.

2. The Superintendent of the University will issue the necessary orders governing the nature and the schedule of courses, and the personnel of directors and teachers. He will act as chairman of the faculties and the military staff whenever they meet in joint session. He will be ex-officio member of the University Council and of all faculties and committees.

3. The chairman of the Army Educational Commission will be the Educational Director of the University. He will act as chairman of the University Council. He will be ex-officio member of all faculties and committees.

4. The Army Educational Commission, in addition to advising the Superintendent of the University as to general educational policies, will recommend to him the appointment of the directors of the colleges and the first heads of

departments. The commissioners will be ex-officio members of the University Council.

5. The University Council will consist of the Superintendent, the educational Director and other members of the Army Educational Commission ex-officio, and of the directors of the various colleges, of the Registrar, and of the head of the Saturday course in citizenship. The Council will recommend to the Superintendent all action governing the nature and schedule of courses, and the personnel of the faculties.

6. The director of each college will recommend to the Council the nature and schedule of the courses given by his faculty, and will nominate its personnel. He will act as chairman of his faculty and ex-officio member of all its departments and committees.

7. The faculty of each college will consist of all its teaching force. At the first meeting of each term, faculties will elect a secretary, an instruction committee, and a schedule committee to serve for the current term. Each faculty will refer to these committees all educational problems of the college, and will meet to discuss or recommend to the director the report of these committees.

8. The secretary of each faculty will keep the minutes of his faculty, and after each meeting will file a copy of the minutes with the record office.

9. The instruction committee of each college, consisting of three members of the faculty and the director ex-officio, will be the executive body of the faculty.

10. The schedule committee of each college will consist of three members and the director ex-officio, and will advise the faculty of the school as to the schedule of classes, of laboratory periods and study hours.

11. A department will consist of all those teaching the same subject. A department may recommend to any faculty

changes in the program of its courses or in its own personnel. The members of a department will nominate to the Council one of their number as chairman of the department.

12. The University Librarian will have charge of all reference libraries and reading rooms of the University.

13. The Registrar of the University will have charge of the registering of the students of the entire school system of the A.E.F.

The First Assistant Registrar will have charge of the registering of students in the A.E.F. University.

The Second Assistant Registrar will have charge of the registering of students in the post and division schools.

The Third Assistant Registrar will have charge of the registering of A.E.F. students in French and British Universities.

By order of Colonel Reeves.

FRANKLIN BABCOCK
Major C.A.C.
Executive Officer

3

Perhaps it was characteristic of Colonel Reeves, the most humane of commanding officers, that when he discovered that Major Babcock would rather study French at Beaune than serve as Executive Officer of the school, he gave him his wish. Major Babcock was a fine chap, popular with all of us, but by temperament a scholar rather than an executive. Major Livingston Watrous took his place.

For the Colonel himself the Beaune episode was decidedly a happy turn of fate. He was a powerful character, middle-aged, with a touch of gray in his hair. He had enlisted in the regular Army while still a boy, and he might have been a professional soldier all his life if education had not exerted over him a peculiar fascination.

He liked to have something to do with a school, the better the school, the better he liked it, but in any case an opportunity to direct the school would lure him away from the command of a regiment, and a fair chance to get into a good war would persuade him to drop education for a command in the line. It so happened that he had missed a complete satisfaction, whether as soldier or educator; his life had fallen within the dates of several wars. He had frequently been wounded, and what with the wounds keeping him out of the fighting, and the fighting interfering with the academic career, he was a baffled, if not disappointed man. General Rees, thoroughly familiar with his record, knew his remarkable executive capacity when he designated him Superintendent of Beaune. He probably knew also that he was giving Reeves at last an opportunity to show his qualities as an educator among men trained to that profession. None of us at Beaune was happier than the Colonel, and no one could be more considerate of his colleagues. His post as military Superintendent might have tempted him to boss the civilian educators around, but nothing could be more correct than his conduct toward us. He and I shared quarters in the same barracks with Major Watrous. Often after we retired for the night we left open the communicating doors of our bedrooms so that we could call out ideas that might come to us for the improvement of the University. He never forgot that the Army Educational Commission were responsible for the purely educational conduct of the school; we were only too glad to leave the military discipline to him.

He was born in Jefferson City, Missouri, in 1872. He enlisted in the Missouri National Guard in 1891. He was commissioned Second Lieutenant with the United States Infantry, April 19, 1897, and served with that regiment during the Santiago campaign, participating in the action at El Caney, San Juan Hill, and Royal Road. For gallantry at El Caney during five days marching and fighting, he was promoted to be First Lieutenant with a handsome citation. February 19, 1899, he left the infantry for the Philippine Islands. He has told me the pleasure he anticipated from the fighting he was sure to get into, but the result of several fierce skirmishes was that the surgeons considered him crippled for life, and he retired from the Army. For a while he served as Commandant and Professor of Military Science, Purdue University, and himself pursued studies in civil engineering. He then served as Commandant and Professor of Military Science at Miami Military Institute, Germantown, Ohio, and at the University of Vermont. In 1915 he was elected President of Norwich University at Northfield, Vermont.

He would have been happy there if the Mexican Border trouble had not broken out. He served on the border as Colonel of the First Vermont Infantry, proving to the medical staff that he had recovered completely from the military adventures. At the outbreak of the First World War he was assigned to inspection duty in Washington, then to the 102nd Infantry in France. In the hard fighting toward the end of the war he found enough action to satisfy him, and on the very day of the Armistice he was severely gassed.

The University at Beaune was set up in what had been, during the war, an American hospital. The Colonel had almost as much experience with hospitals as with schools and garrisons.

This account of his life I take from an official report. The facts, I am sure, could without exaggeration be told more colorfully. At intervals at Beaune he would recall some experience of boyhood and youth which rather opened our eyes.

One noontime when he and I were walking together to the headquarters mess, a truck, through some carelessness on the driver's part, collided with a pole and smashed up one of our soldier-students on his way to lunch. The Colonel and I, seeing the accident, hurried over, but the ambulance arrived almost immediately, and the broken and bleeding body was carried off to the hospital.

At the mess table I had no appetite, and the Colonel guessed the reason.

"You shouldn't let a small thing like that upset you! I began life in a newspaper office. A quart of blood, nowadays, makes no difference one way or another. When I was about fourteen, Father heard of an editor in the next county who wanted a boy to help with the printing press, so I borrowed Father's mule and rode over, to apply for the job.

"The printing press was in a log cabin which served as living room, bedroom, kitchen. There were two bunks against the wall, opposite the front—and only—door. I reached the place just before noon. The editor warmed up some stew, and we had lunch. Then we set type, inked the press, and got out tomorrow's paper, which he had written before I got there. Then we washed most of the ink off our hands, and had supper—more stew. Then he said we'd better turn in, since it was getting dark, and he 'expected a caller. There was a feller who hadn't cared much for what the paper said about him yesterday. I could have the upper berth, the editor would take the lower.

"After that I watched him load his double-barreled gun with buckshot, and after that I fell asleep. Then there was a loud bang! and a bullet whistled halfway between the editor and me.

"'That's him now,' said the editor, and let drive at the caller right through the front door. When everything stayed quiet, the editor opened the door carefully. The caller was lying on his back, with the splinters of the door through him.

"Then the editor drew the bolt again, and slept sound till sunrise. After breakfast we buried the corpse near the door and went on printing."

The Colonel liked the French; he thought he had a peculiar understanding of them.

On the last Sunday of our stay in Beaune, he and I drove in his car to say goodbye to the principal families, particularly to the Marquis and Marquise de Changey. He was a small man with a square beard. His name was Henry. He used the English form. She was fat and merry. Her mother was born in St. Louis, and she had been married twice, each time to a gentleman named the Marquis de Changey. A titled friend from the neighborhood told me what had happened. She was always mischief incarnate; her first husband, much older than she, feared the worst. When he died he left her everything, if she remained a widow. Otherwise she would have only what the law insisted on, and the residue should go to a distant nephew, on condition that the nephew took the name of Changey.

The widow went into heavy mourning for the proper time; then she descended on the nephew and married him.

As we drove near the house we saw three of our soldier-students on the road ahead of us. Their uniforms were pressed, their shoes were polished, they all had a haircut—they had made their preparations for the return voyage to America.

"That's a good sight!" exclaimed the Colonel. "I'm proud of those boys." He stopped his car. "Have you boys ever been inside a French cha-teau?" They never had. "Well, wouldn't you like to see one? Jump in and we'll take you along."

At the Château de Changey the Colonel himself rang the bell, with the soldiers at his heels. The Marquis Henry and the Marquise greeted us in the large front hall, the Marquis Henry looking astonished as usual, and the Marquise bubbling over with hospitable good nature.

"I thought you wouldn't mind if I brought along some of my boys," said the Colonel proudly.

The entrance hall was under a tower, high and four-walled. On each of the walls hung old portraits of ladies and gentlemen in the colorful dress of past days.

"These pictures now," explained the Colonel, "are portraits of Madame's relatives. It's a French custom. They keep pictures of their ancestors right at the door."

The Marquise gave a little scream of delight. "How good of the Colonel! Now I have three more ancestors—two bishops and a cardinal!"

The affection which the soldier-students had for Beaune they owed chiefly to Colonel Reeves. On the first day of registration when troop trains brought them in by the hundreds he made a speech of welcome to each contingent. He reminded them that there must be restrictions on their liberty, since we were still at war, but if they would collaborate he would try to make life at Beaune as happy as on any other campus. So long as they were prompt at drills and their other duties, he would give each one a pass, to leave camp and visit the town of Beaune whenever they were free. After supper that evening the new arrivals, armed with their passes, took a walk down the road to see what Beaune was like.

Next morning Mayor Vincent, unusually perturbed, came hurrying to the Colonel's office. In the bakeries of the town not a cookie remained. Our students, taking their walk—some five thousand of them—had swept through the place like a plague of locusts. It took the Colonel only five minutes to reach a very gratifying understanding with the Mayor. Later in the morning, instead of issuing an order, he talked it over with the boys, and had from them a promise which, so far as I recall, they kept faithfully. They agreed to do their eating at the camp. He promised that the mess would always furnish plenty of "seconds." The Mayor, on his side, pledged the Beaune shopkeepers not to raise prices against the Americans.

Most of the boys used their visits to Beaune as an opportunity to practice their French, especially in the shops where the attendants were good-looking.

When the spring term ended, and General Pershing ordered us all to the west coast for our voyage home, the Colonel insisted on being the last to leave. He made a farewell speech to each trainload, as before he had welcomed them. After one final night in the empty place, he came to Paris, where he and I celebrated the whole adventure with a lunch at La Perrouse. But when our students reached Brest, the ships to bring them home were not ready, and the Army granted them a ten-day furlough to amuse themselves as they chose. Over nine hundred of them went back to Beaune.

4

While we were occupied each with his own work at Beaune it was easy to forget that the busiest department next after the kitchens was probably the Registrar's office. The students who flocked to Beaune by the train-load at the beginning of the term must all be registered; their school records must be noted; their cards must show what courses they were taking, under what teachers. To make their choice of courses possible, a temporary catalog had been printed. Later, a full-size catalog was published in two volumes. Not only the courses of instruction were described, but there was a complete list of students, each with his home address. There was another list of the faculty, each with his academic record and the name of the institution where he had last taught.

Each student selected three courses, any three he wished in any department. The only condition was that the teacher in the course, having examined him, whether formally or informally, was willing to have him in the class. When the term came to an end, or the soldier decided to sail for home with his regiment, he received a certificate stating which three courses he had taken, with the signature of the three teachers, a statement of the number of hours he had attended, and what grade each teacher had given him.

A copy of the complete catalog was sent by the War Department to the Registrar of every college in the United States. The returning student, on presentation of his certificate, could ask for credit on the basis of his record. To estimate the credit, the college authorities had only to consult the Beaune catalog to see the quality of those who had taught him.

To set up a registration office for a university of nearly ten thousand students would be a task under any conditions, but to improvise it with the speed needed to keep up with the mushroom growth of our school at Beaune, would have seemed to me impossible. But we first determined to have a university at Beaune, and afterwards discovered the difficulties. I had never before attempted to administer a university. The problem was mercifully obscured by my inexperience.

When I was gathering teachers in the United States just before the Armistice I did not think how useful a veteran registrar and a well-trained office force could be. But Fate seemed determined that the Beaune venture should have in many directions the quality of what I have called it, a *beau geste*.

Among the well-known educators who enlisted for this work was Dr. Richard Watson Cooper, Secretary of the Association of American Colleges. He had previously been President of Upper Iowa University. No doubt he knew the trials of an institution undersupplied with what it needed. He volunteered to set up the registration machinery. Perhaps he hoped to get free after a week or two and give his time to teaching literature or history, but we never let him go; he was far too useful. And I must add, far too generous. Large in stature, not easily baffled or ruffled by emergencies, he presided over the Registrar's office in a way that was nothing short of noble.

Such a character, born to leadership, attracted to himself naturally a superior group of assistants, of all of whom it can be said, as of him, that perhaps they intended to serve their country in a different way, but they accepted cheerfully the particular task demanded of them.

Dr. Cooper's best assistant, or the one who became best known, was Miss Genevieve Dougine, a teacher of English from the Julia Richmond High School in New York City. With her I remember particularly Miss Catherine Leeds Engle, a bookkeeper from Norfolk, Virginia; Captain Harry Paul Pruner, by profession an auditor; Miss Blanche Mitchell, a statistician who had served on the War Trade Board in Washington; Miss Lillian Beatrice Todd, a secretary in the law firm of Patterson, Eagle, Greenough, and Day, New York; Miss Blanche Lucinda True, head of the department of English Literature at Fargo College, Fargo, North Dakota; and

Miss Mary Hasseltine Vann, Professor of Mathematics at Meredith College, Raleigh, North Carolina.

The usefulness of statisticians and mathematicians in the Registrar's office I should not have understood if I hadn't seen with my own eyes the weird choices which students made, being free to elect any three courses they wanted. In the printed catalog Dr. Cooper reported the number of students in each college, and the number taking each course. By what system of permutations and combinations he and his associates arrived at these results, I cannot say, but I well remember the tier on tier of files containing the registry cards from which the weird statistics were drawn.

One student, as I happen to recall, elected a course in medieval history, a course in landscape painting, and a course in hog-feeding. This meant that he was registered in three colleges—the College of Arts and Sciences, the College of Fine and Applied Arts, and the College of Agriculture. When asked why he chose such ill-assorted subjects, he put us to blush by the good sense of his reply. He had learned a little, very little, about the Middle Ages in high school; but in France during the war, he said, he stumbled over the Middle Ages no matter which way he turned, and he was determined to learn precisely what the Middle Ages were, before he went home.

As to the painting, he had never seen an art museum till after the Armistice. In the Louvre he had found pleasure in landscapes—so much pleasure that he wished he could paint one. He was now taking the course at Beaune to find out whether he had any talent.

As for the hog-feeding, his father had a farm in Iowa, and more than once had mentioned the name of the best expert on hog-feeding in the United States. Perhaps I should say, in his opinion the best expert. Now the son, studying medieval history and landscape painting at Beaune, learned that his father's ideal expert in hog food was also at Beaune, giving a course in his subject. Though the son cared little for hogs and had no intention of feeding them, he elected this course and made careful notes of the lectures. No coming-home gift would please his father more than this record of wisdom from the very source.

5

When once the students were registered a large number of them needed a good library. We had a very good library indeed which we owed to Mr. Luther L. Dickerson, our Librarian, who represented on our campus the American Library Association. Mr. Dickerson had much of Dr. Cooper's equanimity, good nature, and administrative ability. He was a graduate of Oklahoma State Normal School and of New York State Library School. He had served on the Headquarters Staff of the American Library Association at Washington, and had been Librarian of Grinnell University, Iowa. His wide experience included an unusually varied acquaintance with different sections of his own country. A man of wide culture, he was at home in France, and he could act as mediator and interpreter between American students and the foreign conditions in which they sometimes found themselves, even in the friendly landscape of Burgundy.

Mr. Dickerson, like Dr. Cooper, had a large group of assistants. Miss Harriet Catherine Long, his assistant Librarian, was a graduate of the University of Nebraska and the New York State Library School, and she had served as supervisor in the Traveling Library Service for Mexican Border troops. At Beaune she was the Chief Reference Librarian. Miss Pauline Valentine Fullerton, the cataloguer of the Beaune Library, was a graduate of Smith College and of New York State Library School. She had been employed before the war in the Reference department of the New York Public Library. Lieutenant John Lester Feek, superintendent of circulation, was the assistant Librarian of Illinois State Normal University. Mr. Francis Lee Dewey Goodrich, a graduate of the University of Michigan, was Reference Librarian in that institution. Mr. Rudolph

H. Gjelsness, Reference Librarian at Beaune, was a graduate of the University of North Dakota and of the University of Illinois. Before the war he had been Principal of the Adams, North Dakota, High School.

This group, assisted by fifteen others, most of whom Mr. Dickerson found in the Army, provided prompt and expert service for the two thousand readers who during the afternoon and the early evening could be found almost continuously in the barracks which formed our main reading room.

6

Each student, in addition to his three courses five days a week, was required to attend the course in citizenship, presented to the whole University on Saturday morning. Perhaps this was the most original part of the instruction. It was a bold experiment in a field of education, the importance of which is recognized more today than it was in 1919.

The Beaune course every Saturday consisted of an address followed by an hour of discussion and an hour of lantern-slide and motion picture demonstration. The address was prepared in advance, and instructors were drawn from the faculty at large to deliver it during the first hour on Saturday morning, and to conduct the discussion during the second hour in sections of two hundred students each. The third hour, devoted to the motion picture visualization of phases of the subject, was presented to assemblies of about twenty-five hundred students each. The entire course was administered by Lieutenant Colonel William Freeman Snow, graduate of Leland Stanford Jr. University, and Professor of Hygiene and Public Health at that institution.

The successive addresses read to the student body on Saturday morning had the following subjects:

1. The University and its Ideals   Dr. John Erskine
2. The Elements of Citizenship   Dr. H. H. Murphy

3. Vocations, Their Possibilities and Their Limitations — Dr. K. I. Butterfield

4. Social Customs — Dr. R. B. Fosdick

5. The World's Food Supply — Mr. Herbert Hoover

6. City Planning and Community Housing — Mr. Grosvenor Atterbury

7. Industrial Problems — Lt. Col. J. P. Jackson

8. Public Safety and Welfare — Mr. J. A. Kingsbury

9. Public Education — Dr. E. F. Spaulding

10. Public Health — Col. J. H. Ford

11. Art and the Citizen — Mr. George S. Hellman

12. Religion and the Citizen — Bishop Brent

13. Governments and Their Foreign Relations — Dr. Wm. J. Newlin

14. The Heritage of the Future Generation — Mr. Ernest B. Babcock

15. The Principles of Citizenship Applied — Lt. Col. W. F. Snow

7

The late spring of 1919 was warm and bright, and a particularly happy mood fell on the Americans at Beaune. Because we knew our stay in France was short, we began to think of the good we had found there, and forgot the unlovely winter, the stretches of mud and rain. Colonel Reeves was our leader in welcoming the season of light and pleasant blossoms. He encouraged the students to hold regimental dances, and set a good example all over the floor. ("My, but I was light on that girl's feet!") Since the largest rooms available for the dances were floored with concrete, he covered the concrete with wax. I never saw the Colonel worried except once, when General Dawes visited Beaune and asked hard questions about several tons of wax candles which could not be found.

The champion dancers of the University were Major Watrous and Miss Frances Peirce, one of the secretaries in the Educational Director's office. But no one was embarrassed by a comparative lack of skill. Those who knew taught those who didn't, and the Colonel set an example to all, not to let their zeal for perfection spoil the pleasure of the evening.

Over the week-ends we had visitors from Paris and from the various French universities. The rumor of American methods in education reached French teachers everywhere, and when they could take a holiday they dropped in on us and investigated.

In a special class were Professor E. Azambre, from the Sorbonne, and Mr. Theron Crawford, of Paris, one of my best friends in France. Professor Azambre, whose subject was economics, was curious about the life of American students. Like many of his colleagues, he was convinced that the French universities would gain by the addition of sports in the American way, and of the social amusements which American students of both sexes organized for themselves. Before I came to Beaune, Mr. and Mrs. Azambre entertained me most hospitably and very frequently in their home, and plied me with questions about our college life. Late in the spring of 1919 he spent a day at Beaune.

I had some difficulty in making clear to him that football and baseball are not simple pastimes, games to be played at odd moments when you have nothing else to do. The sight of a regimental dance in the evening gave him pleasure, but probably more misinformation than he had ever accumulated in so brief a time. The stenographers and secretaries, dancing with the soldier-students, he was quite sure were what we called in the United States co-eds. Major Watrous and Colonel Reeves, cavorting around the floor, he believed were the Professors of Social Deportment, exercising their pupils.

Between dances students and girls would climb the thirty-foot tower which Colonel Reeves had built near his headquarters for the convenience of visitors who wished a bird's-eye view of the whole camp. The dancers climbed to the top and leaned on the protecting rail in order to cool off. Professor Azambre was a little startled by my attempts to find a sufficiently casual equivalent in French for "cool off."

Mr. Crawford was an elderly newspaper correspondent, wealthy and retired, who had spent his youth in Washington and his comfortable later years in Europe, chiefly in France and Spain. He lived at the Hotel Westminster in the Rue de la Paix. When the Germans threatened to reach Paris, he refused to move out, a decision of which he was permanently proud.

The experiment of the American Army at Beaune was in his opinion one of the most important events in modern times. As possible results from it he foresaw a close linking of the United States with those parts of Europe which he happened to like. Delightful man, he was convinced that Germany would never again amount to a row of pins, but France, especially the southern part near his beloved Pyrenees, would become a favorite resort of all intelligent Americans.

At Beaune he stayed with me at the Headquarters barracks, and took his meals of course at the Headquarters' mess, except for the dinners we had at the Hôtel de la Poste. The Colonel and his officers liked him, and kept to themselves their amusement at the dinner coat he had brought along. "These military chaps like good form. I didn't know how they would dress on this campaign. I didn't want to let you down."

Two other visitors from Paris were Professor William T. Brewster, of Columbia, and Colonel Charles W. Exton, in charge of the students whom we sent to the Sorbonne. Brewster and Exton had much in common. Brewster was still the kindly gentleman with Harvard and Boston ideas whom I had known in my freshman and sophomore years. Exton was graduated from West Point in 1898, served with the Cuban expedition, and afterward for three years in the Philippine Islands, and then for three in the Hawaiian Islands. Then he spent four years as instructor at West Point, and the two and a half years immediately preceding our entry into the First World War, as military attaché in Switzerland. These various contacts with life, instead of bewildering or perplexing his character, had focused it. I can't imagine a wiser commanding officer for the students in Paris, or a better representative of American culture. He and Mr. Brewster understood perfectly what we were doing at Beaune, and noted all the points in which we were succeeding. I had the impression that a sound education, in their judgment, could be had at Harvard, unless you went to West Point—or at West Point, unless you went to Harvard.

8

I cherish two memories of friends and acquaintances made at Beaune and the country around. I think not of their visits to the University but of my visits to them. At Number 4 in the Avenue de la Gare, the long street leading from the center of the town to the station, lived my friend George Dolby. He had a comfortable apartment over a furniture shop in the last block on the left as you came from the station.

He was an Englishman of wide travel and of sound character. I never knew his whole story, but he had arrived at Beaune in his European ramblings with a venerable aunt of whom he was very fond. The aunt fell ill, died, and was buried in the little cemetery, and he settled down for the rest of his life, as it were, to keep watch over her grave. What wealth he had before the war, I don't know, but his apartment was comfortably furnished in a somewhat out-dated fashion. When the American hospital was erected at Beaune, he made himself its unofficial photographer. He had a fine camera and could use it skilfully. After the University occupied the hospital buildings, the Signal Corps made our official records, but George Dolby took many portraits, and we had the impression that he needed to earn the money. He made some really beautiful port-folios of Beaune, the best record I have of the town and its ancient buildings.

Discovering that I liked to play chess, he asked me to his place one evening, and after a fairly interesting game he talked for hours about his life, sending me away at last with the feeling that British bashfulness and reticence had kept from me all the most exciting parts.

He is dead long ago, and rests in the little cemetery beside that mysterious aunt of his. I still ponder the chance that brought so lonely and so charming a spirit to Beaune to meet the unpredictable apparition of our short-lived school.

Miss Caroline McCullagh, the head of my office force, used to say that from her California point of view, however attractive France might be, the French themselves were not a convincing people. When I replied that she'd like them if she knew them, she said she was ready to know them any time.

I asked her to save the late hours one Sunday afternoon for a walk across the countryside. George Hellman and I had chanced on a picturesque farm belonging to a Madame Gauthey, who had invited us in to see the homestead where she as well as her father had been born. Miss McCullagh and I now rang the bell at Madame Gauthey's gate. The old lady showed us the farmyard where the chickens were kept, the rabbits, and the pigs; she pointed out the different fruit trees, the field in in which wheat was grown for her bread-making, the vines from which she pressed her red wine, the other vines which produced the white. She showed us in a massive chest bundles of linen which she had woven for her trousseau. Her husband and her son were both dead, her grandsons had fallen in the First World War, and she was left alone.

Then she showed us the kitchen, where she had been born. I startled her by asking if she wouldn't invite Miss McCullagh and me to have supper with her.

"But there is nothing to eat!"

"Surely, Madame, there are some eggs and bread and cheese?"

"That, of course."

"And perhaps a pint of your red wine?"

She cooked the delicious food for us on the stove which had

warmed her birthplace, all the time talking about the good days when her children were alive, and the world was at peace. She would accept no money for the meal. I asked her to let me send a car and bring her to the University for our next band concert.

"Many thanks, Monsieur, but I don't like music."

"You don't like it?"

"Monsieur, there was a time when I loved it, but now my people are all dead, and it makes me cry."

CHAPTER XI

National Training

TOWARD the close of the university term at Beaune I made this report to General Pershing. With his permission it was published in the *Review of Reviews,* October, 1919.

I wrote the report of my own volition, with no prompting from my military colleagues. It expressed my own ideas. Dr. Spaulding held much the same views. President Butterfield disagreed entirely, fearing that the entry of the Army into the educational field would militarize the American mind.

I reprint the report here because the question of national training is once again in our minds, and the educational principles upon which the report is based seem more than ever valid.

1

No problem now before the United States is more important than the question of national education. Even while we were preparing for war, we had occasion to feel some alarm at certain weaknesses in our educational system revealed by those preparations. At the same time, so amazed were we at the resourcefulness of our national character in times of stress, that we asked why our great national reserves of intelligence and skill should not be mobilized more completely in times of peace for the constant good of the country. Now that the war is passed we find ourselves facing the special problem of training for national defense. Some kind of Army we must have, large or small, and some kind of training. Shall we give this training solely to a group of professional soldiers? Shall this training look only to the contingencies of war?

Some of us who have been working with our fellow citizens on foreign soil and from that distance have looked back toward our country, studying it with increased affection and perhaps also with increased concern, earnestly hope that our people will train for national defense, and that they will interpret national defense in a larger way than any nation has yet thought of. We have in mind, of course, the total needs of American education—the need of more and better schools, the need of large revisions in college and university curricula, the need of a strong national department of education. For the moment, however, we have in mind particularly the defects of education observed in the United States Army in France, and also what the educational program in the American Expeditionary Forces has done to remedy those defects; and since we are convinced that the time has arrived for all progressive nations to organize for peace as well as for war, conceiving of national defense as preparation for peace and war, we would address ourselves for the moment to the specific problem of national training.

The principles according to which we would envisage such national training are five. In the first place, the idea of universal service should be expanded so as to include training for all other duties of citizenship besides military, and to include training of all prospective citizens, even of those physically unfit for military service. In the second place, the present temporary cantonments in the United States, or equivalent cantonments, should be converted at once into permanent training schools for citizenship. In the third place, a permanent educational corps should be added to the Army. This corps should be formed of the most competent experts in school, in vocational, and in the more elementary college subjects.

From time to time competent officers in other branches of Army service should be assigned to this corps. In the fourth place, there should be a compulsory training period of twelve months with the colors, from September 1 to September 1, or from June 1 to June 1, or between any other dates which should be found practical, care being taken simply to fit this period into other educational or vocational obligations. This period should fall between the ages approximately of 18 to 20, perhaps a little earlier or a little later, as experience might prove advisable. Approximately one-half of this training should be for military science and for physical development, the other half for training under military discipline in school, in vocational, or in college subjects. In the fifth place, the citizen in training should be free to elect the kind of civil education he receives, with the exception that training in elementary subjects should be compulsory for illiterates and for the foreign-born.

The mobilization of the American Army demonstrated that an astounding number of native-born citizens are illiterate, and that of our foreign-born citizens a still larger number cannot read or write the English language; and in some cases cannot understand it. The mobilization demonstrated also that an appalling number of our young men are not in proper physical condition. It is unliikely that any economic or social pressure will tend to remedy these evils. The illiterate citizen can make a living of a sort more or less satisfactory to himself, and both classes can avoid that social criticism which would urge them toward complete citizenship. In fact, economic and social pressure tends actually to segregrate in our country the illiterate element and the various groups of foreign-born, and unless some strenuous effort is made to weld all these groups into one, there is no likelihood of change in these unfortunate conditions.

The program of education in the American Expeditionary Forces has demonstrated, on the other hand, that even brief courses of study, followed intensively under military discipline, are adequate to correct illiteracy and to teach our language. The whole experience of our Army demonstrates further that if brought together in a common purpose the various elements of our population can be speedily amalgamated. We should now find a means to provide these benefits for our country in time of peace.

Even those soldiers who are neither illiterate nor unable to command the English language showed to a distressing degree the inefficiency of our population education. The men waiting to return to the United States were pathetically eager to master some trade or some profession in order to be sure of a worthy place in the society to which they were returning. Far more than one-half of the American Expeditionary Forces are without adequate training for any trade or profession, and, perhaps because of the intellectual stimulus of their experiences in the war, they are uncomfortably aware of their lack. It is disturbing to think that they may miss their proper place in their generation. It is more disturbing to reflect, however, that even had they not come to Europe in the Army they would still have been without training for professions or trade; in fact, through the Army educational program they are now accidentally receiving such training in preparation for citizenship as is provided nowhere in the United States for any large group of men. It seems folly not to make permanent in our national life for all citizens the advantages which many soldiers now temporarily enjoy.

The mobilization of our Army has shown, on the other hand, how rich potentially the manhood of our nation is, and how quickly it responds to the regular life and scientific care which even a hurried preparation for war supplied. The soldiers in general enjoyed such health as is the rule in no other community. The total discipline of their life—regular hours, rational diet, and decorum of conduct—has brought out their best physical and moral traits and has quickened to the full their intellectual capacities, so that those who have taught them in all subjects from the most elementary to the most advanced have wondered at their eagerness and ability to learn.

Furthermore, the life in the Army has developed in our youth a sense of social cooperation which some of us feared was lacking in the American character. No body of men in our country seems now more eager to study and to deal intelligently with the social problems which confront us than the men of the Army, who have been learning in a kind of laboratory course what responsibility each of us owes to his fellow. The fact that in the Army they met other Americans from all parts of the country has developed a new sense of nationality; and the meeting in the same ranks of rich and poor has developed a new sense of democracy. These advantages of health and morale, of intellectual awakening, of patriotism, and of democratic sympathy we desire to provide for each generation in our country, and as much for those who are never called into battle as for those who in times of the nation's need answer the call.

It is the logic of our course in this war that our Army, organized to defend the ideals of civilization, is now proving itself to be a vast university of citizenship. It would be the most profitable result of the war for our country and for the world should this university in citizenship become permanent for all our people.

This training should be provided for all men not mentally deficient. Even those who are physically unfit for military service can derive great benefits from such bodily training as is suited to their needs, and quite as much as other men can derive benefit from training in the non-military duties of citizenship. Much of the disrupted thinking in society is done by men physically handicapped, whose point of view toward their fellows is warped or embittered by their own misfortune. In many cases their philosophy of life would be made more generous by an improvement in their health, and in all cases society owes it to them to provide even more adequate advantages than for those who start life without handicap. Association with their fellow citizens in a national system of training would probably develop in these men at least a greater sense of unity with the nation and increase of pride in what they themselves could contribute to society as a whole. In a very large number of cases the physical defects which now handicap the youth of our country can be easily corrected; but, like illiteracy, they can be corrected only if society insists on bringing the individual under the proper course of training.

The advantage of converting the present training cantonments or equivalent cantonments into permanent training schools is obvious. In our country much sentiment attaches to places of education, and if we are to install in our national life a vast system of training in citizenship, it is in our temper to make of those places where this citizenship is taught shrines, as it were, of affection. If men look back with reverence to their college campus or to the school in which they first had some glimpse of the possibilities of life, there is reason why these large schools should be far more deeply revered in which men from whole sections of the country will be brought together for training in the total defense of their homes—in the defense of their country against possible enemies on sea or land, against disease, ignorance, and incompetency.

In these permanent schools much of the equipment now used for purposes of war could be used constantly for purposes of peace. The materials which in time of war must be gathered hurriedly, instruments for engineering, for chemical research, for hospital and sanitary service, would be maintained at the highest point of excellence in the laboratories of these schools. At the American Expeditionary Forces University at Beaune, the laboratories in chemistry, physics, bacteriology, medicine, biology, engineering, fine arts, and music have been supplied largely out of the resources of the Army. On the return of the Army to the United States it would be in the highest degree desirable if these laboratories could continue to serve educational purposes, and other laboratories also on a much larger scale, which would then be available at short notice for any emergency in national defense.

If it is desirable to maintain for permanent uses the material which our Army temporarily collects for war, it is still more desirable to retain for the advantage of our country in times of peace the educational resources which the Army must also improvise for war. A part of the duty of the modern army involves scholarship of high order, knowledge of languages, of history, of international politics, and, of course, of the sciences. A nation which trains for all the duties of citizenship, civil as well as military, will find it advantageous to develop in peace times the scholarship that can be useful in war.

In the schools here described, experts would be needed to teach all elementary and secondary school subjects, trades and vocations, and such subjects of college or university grade as the youth in training would be qualified to pursue. In addition to the experts who would form the nucleus of this educational corps, teachers should be recruited from officers in other branches of Army service, who from time to time would thus have an opportunity to exercise their own scholarship and to make a direct contribution to the intellectual and social life of the country. Hitherto it has been only by accident that armies have been permitted to do constructive social work; after a war with Cuba, for example, the army surgeon is permitted to clean up a fever district. There is no reason why the training of engineers, or surgeons, or officers in every branch of the service should not at all times be at the disposal of the country.

It will be noted that in the period of training the proportion of non-military education is approximately equivalent to the amount of time required to study yearly in the average high school or college. The time, therefore, spent in national training would not be in addition to the years required for higher education. The period of training is so situated between high school and college that those young men, the comparatively few of our country, who enjoy a college education, can during the year of service cover the ground of their freshman work and can also learn habits of application and of study at the moment when they most need to learn them. In fact, it is not impossible that the months spent in the unusually favorable conditions of regular hours and good health will save time for the average student.

No one familiar with college life is blind to the fact that college students ordinarily waste the greater part of their time. This is true even if one admits that an important benefit of college life is the social contact established with other men of one's age. It is not so generally realized that the average college student is extremely careless in his diet and, on the whole, is far below the physical state in which at his age he should be. It has been the hope of college athletics to correct this deplorable condition but in this hope we have been disappointed. Army life, however, as this war has demonstrated, provides for every soldier a finer system of training than athletes usualy submit themselves to in times of peace. The student in perfect health will waste less time in idleness and will make greater progress when he does study, than the average college boy as we have known him.

Obviously we must teach the illiterate to read and write, and we must teach the foreign-born to use our language. Aside from this obligation, however, an essential feature of national training should be the complete liberty of the man trained to select his studies. The nation should undertake during the year of training to advance him as far as possible in any course of study which he desires and is equipped to follow. If he looks forward to business, to agriculture, to industry, then this training should help him toward that career. If he expects to attend college, the training should take the place of his freshman year. If he desires to study art, his training should be in art.

Experience with the educational program in the American Expeditionary Forces demonstrates almost unthought of potentialities in the American character. Our soldiers apparently have as great native endowments in the arts as the most favored of the Latin races, and a system of national training which should try to develop all of the latent powers of the individual would shortly transform our national life. Perhaps the temptation of any such system as we are here suggesting would be to prescribe for youth what it should study. This temptation must be absolutely avoided. To yield to it would be to overwhelm the whole country in that form of intellectual Prussianism which now fortunately is found only in the conservative catalogs of some of our universities—those who persist in prescribing subjects which are dead or in teaching vital subjects as though they were dead. Beyond this suggested system of national training the universities should still pursue their work of teaching and research, functioning according to their special facilities. But the nation should undertake to make an inventory of its citizenship in each generation, and to advance every man as far as possible toward the work to which he feels called.

Such a system of training as is here suggested would be expensive. The items of expense would be buildings and their upkeep, their equipment, the teachers who would form the framework of the educational corps, and the cost of providing subsistence for the men in training. All these expenses, however, should be charged frankly to national education, and we should realize that in one form or another this outlay is unavoidable. We may refuse to combat illiteracy and disease, we may refuse to assume responsibility for the making of the foreign elements in the United States into a unified nation; but in that case we shall pay for the support of poorhouses, of hospitals, of jails, and of police, and we shall pay even more heavily in loss of national health and efficiency. If we are to check the ignorance, the disease, and the discontent which in various ways menace our society, we must be ready to pay as much for education as we are now prepared to invest in international canals or in war bills.

It is a tendency of our country to disguise the cost of education. We remit taxes on educational buildings and on lands devoted to educational purposes, and in our bookkeeping we distribute the cost of tuition. Yet even when the whole account is shown, it does not appear that we give generously to education, though as a nation we have enjoyed a reputation for doing so. Until we are ready to pay for popular education we are not likely to achieve even approximately those minimum results which we sometimes try to make ourselves believe we are reaching. In order to give even one year of sound training to every young man in our country, it will be necessary to assume the cost as a national expense. There should, of course, be some financial return to the country in the greater efficiency of our citizens and in the decrease of disease and irresponsibility. But whether or not such a result does follow, the nation should be asked now to face the internal peril of illiteracy and of ignorance as frankly and as generously as it faced the menace of an enemy from abroad.

A system of training so organized would have obvious advantages. The annual inventory of our educational shortcomings would point out for our school system the task to which it should address itself. Undoubtedly the result would be that year by year the schools would send to the training camps generations better prepared; by keeping the election of the courses in the training camps entirely free we should assist each student to make progress from the point at which his civilian education had been interrupted, and the gradual rise of standards in this year of training would be a barometer of national progress intellectually. The year of training would also show which parts of the country were providing inadequate facilities for education, and means could be taken by the national government to improve the schools in those districts. It is not unlikely that as a result of this national training and of the statistics which it would make available, the nation would soon be persuaded, as it should have been persuaded long ago, to establish in the federal government a strong department of education, and that department would collaborate with the Army in training for citizenship.

But the most direct advantage would be for the large majority of our young men who at present receive no high school training at all, nor even much elementary education. To insure for them a reasonable start in life would be worth any cost and any effort. In no other way than by national training, undertaken as a national expense, can this vast body of each generation be sought out in the small town, on the farm, in the overcrowded city, and can be taught the things essential to each individual case. To care for this neglected majority would be really to train our nation.

Perhaps the by-product of such a system of training as is here out-lined would be the bringing of the Army into a sane relation with society. Through the fear of militarism which possesses the modern world it has become our custom to support the Army and to admire military science only in moments of extreme need. As a result, the soldier in war time receives an adulation perhaps exaggerated and in peace times he is neglected, feared, certainly put to no good use. At this moment, when our Army thinks of returning, it is interesting to consider that every man in it hopes to go back to some constructive work for his country, except the professional soldier. He can look forward only to inactivity until the spasmodic need of him arises again. Perhaps society is wise in fearing the Army which has noth-ing to do; it is stupid in finding no use for the Army in time of peace. If we could add to the military functions of our Army the constructive kind of national defense, we should be providing a noble and honored career for the man on whom in extreme mo-ments the life of the nation depends; we should be bringing the soldier into constant relation with the social needs of the country he serves, and we should be teaching every youth within our borders John Milton's large conception of citizenship, "I call therefore a complete and generous education that which fits a man to perform justly, skillfully, and magnanimously, all the offices, both private and public, of peace and war."

2

When I published this paper twenty-one years ago the social con-science of the United States was not yet roused, and we were not yet accustomed to the expenditure of large sums for the wholesale benefit of human beings. I admitted in this article that though the plan could be carried out by the Army at a minimum cost, the total sums needed would be large. Today, if I were rewriting the piece, I would face about and try to reassure the taxpayer in complete sincerity that this educational plan, by preparing us for the emer-gencies of peace as well as of war, would take the place of much well-meaning but aimless and expensive effort to relieve unemployment. We spend billions to relieve distress without much guarantee that those who are temporarily relieved are permanently helped, or to any degree put in a position to help themselves. In contrast, this plan for national training begins to look even more economical and practical than I first thought it.

But though it would be, I believe, a substitute for relief, I think of it not as a mere remedy for social inequities, but as a positive opportunity even for those who are born in good fortune. I wish every boy in the country could have this training at the end of his high school course, or at the age he would have reached had he gone to high school. I wish all our young men could meet at least for that one year on terms of absolute democracy. I should like to see the young conservative bunking in with the young radical. Whatever became of their theories later, they would know each other as human beings. I should like the boys from one section of the country to do their year of service in another section. I should expect that those who after this year of service went on to college, would go with a maturity of mind which is not at present noticeable in freshmen. After the service year a boy should be qualified to enter the sophomore class.

When I published this paper originally I had my share of abuse for thinking so well as I do of the Army. I was told that my plan would be a dangerous instrument in the hands of the militaristic. My experience, however, is that in our country, where the Army is not considered a class career, there are probably more militaristic minds in civilian groups than among our trained officers. If we wish to encourage militarism, the surest way to do it is to make available for officers none but wartime occupations. But the soldier, it should be remembered, has given us the ideal of chivalry as well as the threat of militarism. In a civilized society, I believe, the army will never be abolished. I wish it might some day be called upon to defend the country against that ignorance and that lack of opportunity which are the internal enemy. The citizen who has health and a fair chance, with full play for his mind, is likely to have good humor also, and the spirit of comradeship and helpfulness, without which no society can hold together.

3

In 1940 or slightly later Colonel Eugenio Silva, of Cuba, called on me in my New York home. To my surprise and great pleasure he had come on my report years before, and cherished a well-worn copy of the *Review of Reviews* in which it first appeared. Being in Washington on a special mission for his country, he looked me up to tell of a magnificent expansion of my idea which he was advocating at every opportunity among his friends in Central and South America. His dream is a year of national training in every country in the hemisphere, including Canada. The training would be as I have described, civilian studies in camps under army discipline, to serve the needs of peace as well as war. But Colonel Silva wants the trainees in each American country to acquire two languages besides his own. The camps in the United States would teach Spanish and Portuguese, in Cuba Portuguese and English, in most South American countries the same, and in Brazil Spanish and English.

While the war was on, Colonel Silva worked hard for his idea, and though the actual progress he made was virtually nothing, yet many in high office everywhere approved, and it may well be that in time the idea of combining civilian education with universal military training may take root—in Latin America.

I wish I could be optimistic about the establishment of such training in the United States. We need, and it seems now that we may have, universal military training, but the experiment at Beaune is not even a memory to most of our people, and civilian educators, most schoolteachers and college professors, like to say that peacetime and wartime subjects cannot be taught together. I can think of no sillier objection. If they have forgotten Beaune, at least they should remember the academies at West Point and Annapolis. In both of these schools for war the cultural subjects are well taught, languages, history, geography, mathematics, economics. In addition the students receive a physical training and a drill in manners and etiquette that starts them off in life with an advantage over most college graduates. My hope for this combined training for all American boys will probably disturb no college in its intrenched privilege of incompetence.

Do I seem to speak too harshly of the colleges? I don't see how they can bring the charge, not until this generation forgets that in the hour of national peril the greatest service the colleges could render was to turn over their buildings and equipment to Army or Navy, so that what were called "refresher courses" might be installed—in plain words so that effective instruction might be given in essential subjects which until war came the colleges had skimped. Mathematics, for example.

Every college teaches mathematics, and most of them would insist that they teach it well. But in college the student is not required to master a subject. Seventy-five per cent is a passing mark. Though this is college, it isn't life. It certainly isn't war. If you order a four-wheeled vehicle and I bring you a wagon with one wheel missing, you will not give me a passing mark. The three-quarters kind of accomplishment is tolerated only in the liberal college. Liberal indeed!

CHAPTER XII

Great Books

1

IN 1917, just before America entered the war, fully half my teaching was in undergraduate courses, and I was working out a number of ideas about the presentation of great authors and their works to young people, normally and properly occupied with contemporary life.

It was the fashion among many of my older colleagues to refer with regret, and certainly not with respect, to the literary ignorance of the younger generation. They might do very well in the courses we gave on American and English literature, but they knew little or nothing, said their critics, about the Bible, or Homer, or Vergil, or Dante, or the other giants whom the world at large has long esteemed. This opinion of undergraduate ignorance was often expressed with the implication that if the boys and girls knew little about the great books, a deterioration had set in since their fathers and mothers went to school.

I doubted whether the elders in general, even among college professors, spent much more time than the youngsters reading world classics, but if the faculty believed that the boys in college ought to be familiar with more than the titles of great books, that happy result could be achieved in a new kind of course, extending through two years, preferably the junior and senior years, and devoted to the simple principle of reading one great book a week, and discussing it in a weekly meeting which would last two or three hours.

I announced this opinion with vigor during an otherwise dull faculty meeting. I reminded my colleagues that the *Iliad* and most other epics were shorter than the average novel, and many of our students read at least one popular novel every seven days. Having read a new book, which their dormitory mates were also reading, they would then engage in a hot discussion about it. Why not treat the *Iliad,* the *Odyssey,* and other masterpieces as though they were recent publications, calling for immediate investigation and discussion? After two seasons of this kind of reading, Columbia boys would have an acquaintance with world literature from all countries, and not simply poetry and fiction. Certainly we should read the great books of ancient and modern scientists and philosophers.

Nobody who knows what a college faculty is like will jump to the conclusion that my proposal was greeted with applause. I was told that to read Homer in translation would be the same thing as not reading Homer at all. Even a two-hour discussion of a great writer would be inadequate for a scholarly grasp of him. I agreed. I couldn't help adding that I marveled at my colleagues who did their reading exclusively in the original. I publicly offered them my sympathy for never having read the Old Testament, nor the words of Christ. Of course the Old Testament was possible for any colleague who knew Hebrew, but there was no text extant of the words of Christ in the language he spoke.

The faculty rejoinders were rather warm. I suggested that we should remember the wide difference between a reading acquaintance with great authors, and a scholarly investigation of them. The original charge against the younger generation was not their lack of scholarship, but their reluctance to read great books. The audience who thronged the ancient theatre to enjoy a new work by Aeschylus or Sophocles were not classical scholars; they were merely the human beings for whom the play was written. I added, not at all tactfully, that the lectures of scholarly classicists sometimes ignore the fact that the Greek dramatists wrote plays for human beings.

How seriously my Great Books plan was opposed by some of my colleagues may be illustrated by the following letter to Dean Keppel. The writer was not much older than I, we were colleagues and contemporaries, meeting every day as we came and went from our classes. He never criticised my plan openly in faculty meetings. He never mentioned it to me favorably or otherwise. As his letter states, he did not attend the special meeting at the old Faculty Club which the Dean called for a frank discussion. I imagine that Keppel passed the letter on to me because he himself had doubts of my proposal, and wished the opposition to be heard.

> I have been giving some thought to the proposed required courses in the college for the two years preceding graduation, as outlined in the *Gazette* for January. I realise that I have no voice in legislation for the college, as I do not sit on that Faculty, but since I have given Senior and Junior work in the college for the past ten years, I am writing you informally to express my entire disapproval of the plan.

> I see various practical difficulties, but I shall limit my criticism to what seems to me to be the main issue,—that an ambitious program like this can lead only to a smattering of knowledge, and not to a real understanding of any one author. It is proposed, for instance, to instruct the student in Dante, Aristo, Rabelais, Tasso, Cervantes, Shakspere, Calderon and Corneille in a single half-year, during which time he is to complete an equally elaborate list in history, and another in philosophy, to say nothing of other academic activities of his Senior year, in the curriculum and elsewhere. When is he to eat and sleep? How much real grasp will he get of any of these authors? He can, of course, devote only a very limited amount of time to each.

I know by experience with these same men how long it takes them to acquire a real understanding of Shakspere, a far easier classic for English-speaking people than Dante or Calderon, and I know from having given outline courses to undergraduates elsewhere the dangers of trying to teach too many things at once. I feel that the results of any such plan will be most unfortunate for true scholarship in Columbia College, that if that institution is to make a choice, it should stand for exact knowledge of a few things rather than for superficial acquaintance with many things. I firmly believe that it is better that a man should get to know ten authors well in his last two years in college, than that he should learn the names of the eighty-four men presented to him on this list, for I doubt if he would learn much more.

I regret very much that I was not present at the recent meeting of the Faculty Club; an unexpected and pressing engagement detained me. While I realize the admirable motives that underlie this scheme, I cannot refrain from making an energetic protest against it.

The war cut short our argument, but after I returned from Beaune and we resumed our teaching in the autumn of 1919, I asked the College faculty for authorization to try out the Great Books course, beginning in 1920.

It immediately became clear that the faculty could not define a great book; at least they couldn't agree on a definition. Worn out by futile talk, the Committee abandoned the task and told me to go ahead in my own way. The permission was granted in a tone which seemed to say, "And may God have mercy on your soul!"

After the course had been given for a while, it would have been easier for us all to define a great book. The discussion method which I was proposing paralleled closely that which society gives to every book as it first appears. A great book is one that has meaning, and continues to have meaning, for a variety of people over a long period of time. The world chooses its great books by a social process. I wanted the boys to study great books by the same social process—by reading them simultaneously and by exchanging opinions about them. Some books, of course, attract only readers and admirers of a special temperament; in my opinion these are not great books, and it's no use trying to study them socially. They are best handled by an individual professor in a lecture, after which no questions, protests or back-talk will be encouraged. I am here thinking of two extremely interesting women writers, resembling each other chiefly in strength of will and in self-sufficiency—Amy Lowell and Gertrude Stein.

The really great writers have been accepted by large groups of people for many different reasons. The English admire Shakespere, so do the Germans and so do the French, but each national temperament admires a different Shakespere. In the course on Great Books, when we ask the students why a given play of Shakespere's seems great to them, though they know nothing about the German, French, Italian or British critics, they may express sincerely and instinctively one of those points of view, having discovered it not in books but in their own temperament. Exchanging ideas for two hours, they will probably teach each other more about the rich aspects of Shakespere's genius than any one of them is likely to think out for himself, or than any lecture is likely to convey.

After the students have read and discussed the author of the week they share a body of literary information and opinion which serves for future conversation and argument. Perhaps for the first time they have the basis for an intellectual life in common. Meeting on the campus they need not confine their talk to estimates of athletic prowess or to school gossip. The great writers provide, as Wordsworth said they would, nobler loves and nobler cares.

For more intimate discussion we divided the Columbia class into sections of twenty-five or thirty. All sections met simultaneously on Wednesday evenings. With each group there were two instructors, selected for their disposition to disagree with each other. They were present, not to lecture nor in any way to behave like professors, but to add fuel when necessary to the argument. Few sections stopped talking before the janitor closed the building.

In many places the course has been misunderstood and misapplied. Some colleges give lectures on our list of books instead of discussing them. Lectures may be inspiring or otherwise useful, but they have no place in the natural social approach to literature, as I understand that approach.

Any list of great books will resemble strongly any other list. It was not our purpose at Columbia to name the hundred best books, or anything of the kind. We made as sure as possible that each book was great—that it had proved itself so rich in content that many valid opinions had been held, and could still be held, about it. The books so chosen were discussed chronologically.

The course was not intended as a substitute for specialized study. In particular, it was not meant to discourage the study of languages. Many of our boys, having found out the kind of book the ancients could write, registered for courses in Greek and Latin. This result gave me pleasure, though it was not the purpose of the course to revive the study of the ancient languages. I fear the teachers of Greek and Latin, if they derived any satisfaction from the slight increase in the number of their students, derived the wrong kind of satisfaction. They thought, perhaps, that the way they taught their subject had at last won some small measure of popularity. Or perhaps they imagined that the students, having enjoyed Homer and Vergil through the handicap of the English language, were now eager to revel in the untainted original exactly as the professors of Greek and Latin reveled in their moments of inspired leisure.

It's a queer obsession, this persuasion that all books are best when read in the original. I dare say that from time to time there will continue to be protests against permitting world literature to spread itself in translation. I should rather crusade against lectures by professors who have no gift for lecturing, and against even brilliant lectures on books which are not great.

2

The course in Great Books will be successful only if it is given by teachers who believe in it. During the first year of the Columbia experiment the instructors and junior professors who conducted the discussions were a remarkable lot—Mortimer J. Adler, Raymond M. Weaver, Emery E. Neff, Mark Van Doren, H. W. Schneider, Rexford G. Tugwell, Arnold Whitridge, Henry Morton Robinson, Clifton Fadiman, Irwin Edman, C. W. Keyes, J. Bartlet Brebner. The staff changes with the years, but a tradition soon establishes itself, if the teachers are well chosen from the start.

I think the marks of a good teacher for this course are two; he must believe in what he is doing, and he must have a personal philosophy. Unless great books are our very life, unless we look forward hungrily to the next opportunity to read them ourselves or to hear our students discuss them, unless by impulse and choice we are turning them over in our mind as we walk across the campus or through the school hallways, it is only a cold dish we are likely to serve up to our pupils, and they, taking their cue from us, will discuss great and noble ideas at low temperature and on a low plane.

I might as well add in plain terms, though the thought is somewhat out of fashion, that the successful teacher of the great books of Western Europe for the last two or three thousand years, must have some form of religious philosophy. At the very least he must believe in a spiritual life, he must assume in every human being a soul. This minimum faith may have a Catholic background, a Protestant, or a Jewish. Even the pagan religions of antiquity took account of the soul as well as the body. It is impossible to interpret the masterpieces of the last three thousand years by impoverished philosophies which define man as a biological or chemical accident, or as the by-product of economic forces.

I hold that neither literature nor any of the arts can be understood in the heart as well as the mind, without a spiritual philosophy. Leave out the soul, and the music of Palestrina, of Sebastian Bach or Beethoven, even of composers lesser but still great, like César Franck, must fall on deaf ears. And unless we have spiritual insights and well-developed spiritual emotions, we had better say as little as possible about what Michelangelo put on the ceiling of the Sistine Chapel.

3

In the quarter of a century since the Great Books course was established at Columbia many other colleges have adopted it, and the vitality of this method of study is now generally recognized. Three institutions have connected themselves with it, to an extent not likely to be forgotten—Columbia University, where the idea began, St. John's College at Annapolis, where Stringfellow Barr and Scott Buchanan made it the backbone of the curriculum, and the University of Chicago, where Mortimer Adler and Robert M. Hutchins gave it the vitality of their own personal enthusiasm. In all these institutions, and especially at Chicago, the discussion of great books has been carried outside the academic campus and made accessible to adults in voluntary classes among miscellaneous working groups.

In 1947 a number of those who had watched this adult education at Chicago realized that the University could not be responsible for a project which promised to include very shortly an estimated twenty thousand adult students in seventeen American cities and Vancouver, British Columbia. The Great Books Foundation was established at Chicago. This organization, with a board of eleven directors drawn from education and business, proposed to take over the community programs concerned with the study of great books which the University of Chicago had begun experimentally three years before. Robert M. Hutchins, Chancellor of the University, was granted leave of absence to guide this experiment in adult education, and Lynn A. Williams, Jr., Vice-President of the Stewart-Warner Corporation, was granted leave of absence to be President and active head of the new Foundation. For the previous two years he had organized group discussions of great books among employees of the Stewart-Warner company in Indianapolis.

The novelty of this kind of adult education is obvious, and its possible consequences need no emphasis. Any group of people, old or young, can study books by discussing them. There have been reading circles in many places which never heard of adult education nor of the Great Books program. But discussion may be aimless or futile. It is an advantage to have in each group one or two persons who can keep the talk going in a profitable direction. Such leaders have been trained during the summer of 1947, in Chicago, New York, and elsewhere. They are not professional teachers, nor are they chosen because of any scholastic reputation; rather, they are selected for an interest in books and life, a certain alertness of mind, and a forceful personality. Otherwise it seems desirable that these discussion groups should be homogeneous, with all the members on approximately the same cultural level.

Obviously these discussion groups, amounting to thousands of readers, will need cheap editions of the great books. Such editions are in existence, the Everyman Library, for example, and the publishers cooperate with the Great Books Foundation by printing more copies to take care of the newly created demand.

In October, 1943, Mr. Hutchins wrote me as follows:

The Encyclopaedia Britannica, which is now affiliated with the University of Chicago, has asked me to be general editor of a set of the Great Books of the Western World to be published, if possible, in about two and one-half years.

I should like to have an editorial advisory board whose duty it would be to criticize by conference and correspondence the list, texts, translations, and any other matters arising in the progress of the work. Since you are the father of this kind of study in the United States, I have thought first of you. The others who have occurred to me are Mortimer Adler, Stringfellow Barr, Scott Buchanan, Clarence Faust, Dean of the College at the University of Chicago, Sir Richard W. Livingstone, Joseph Schwab, biologist, who has been in charge of this kind of work in our University College, and Mark Van Doren.

Other members were later added to this Committee. For the next year and a half numerous meetings in New York or Chicago were devoted to very much the same kind of discussion which delayed the original selection of the great books for the Columbia course. There was a natural tendency, as there would be among any professors, to attach extraordinary importance to some titles and to slight others. It is apparently difficult even for wise teachers to realize that literature, being an art, involves questions of personal taste, and that even a personal taste with which we do not agree may have much to be said for it.

I greatly enjoyed the meetings of this Committee which I was able to attend. It was a strange and stimulating experience to be working again with Mortimer Adler and Mark Van Doren over the organization of a Great Books course, and to realize that they, who had once seemed, and still seem, youthful pupils, were now mature men, colleagues of experience and wide influence.

I am still amazed that my simple suggestion for studying great books by the most natural of all methods should have led us so far. If voluntary groups of adults choose to read by this method, they can readily supplement any education they have, or mend any ignorance they are likely to be conscious of.

But it will be a new calamity in our culture if we assume that these discussion classes can be any more than an introduction to books. Science in the Middle Ages could be studied on the page; now scientific progress is made in the laboratories. To ask boys and girls in college, or adult students off the campus, to waste time retracing the literary gropings of outdated science, is in my opinion ridiculous if not criminal.

On the other hand, many a scientist of rank was also a literary artist, and should be read as such. My favorite literary scientist is Hippocrates, who says things about healing which doctors still say, but not always so well.

CHAPTER XIII

What Is a Doctor of Philosophy?

THIS was once an educational question, but it has acquired sociological and economic implications, and it begins to be of interest to anthropologists.

The doctorate of philosophy may occur in either sex. The characteristics or symptoms are constant. The patient writes Ph.D. after his name. No one mistakes him for a physician or for a philosopher, but with the professorial brand on him he will obtain more easily a teaching post in the schools and colleges which are not sure of themselves. Even though he had no Ph.D. the strong institutions might engage him because of his scholarship or his teaching ability, but the timid and self-suspecting would no more permit him to conduct a class without his sacred letters than without his other clothing.

In this superstition there is a grain of hard sense. When a student has finished his school course he receives a diploma, as evidence that he is educated. Why should we not do as much for the professor? He needs a testimonial which is portable and readily displayed. The simple addition of Ph.D., after Smith or Brown, will be accepted anywhere as evidence that some university has tried to make a professor out of him, and nobody so far is dissatisfied with the product. He may not yet have taught anything to anybody, but the university which trained him can't think of a reason why he shouldn't. Unless he has this impressive endorsement the people to whom he applies for employment will have to try him out and make up their own mind, but this they would rather not do, since there are no standard methods for judging a bare teacher without letters.

The letters, be it understood, certify that Smith or Brown is probably fit to teach, but they don't say what. The medieval Doctor was at home in logic and theology, the modern Doctor is more at home in medicine, but the Ph.D. is a sort of blank check which may be filled out by the finder and presented at any institution disposed to take a chance. If you wish you may of course be a Doctor of Philosophy in philosophy, or a Doctor of Philosophy in English, or a Doctor of Philosophy in history, or in economics, or in architecture, or in hygiene, or in cooking, or in football coaching.

The process of acquiring a Ph.D. for teaching purposes is in all cases the same. The candidate first goes to college and collects a diploma, which indicates that he or she is educated in the rough though not yet refined or sharpened to a point. The very essence of cultural education is that at the end of four college years the student shall not know anything in particular. Specialization begins with the fifth year, when the student may apply himself attentively to a few of the things he was supposed to learn in college. At the end of this fifth year he receives another diploma, and becomes a Master of Arts or a Master of Science. He may now proceed to take his Ph.D. unless he prefers to get married. In that case he will begin teaching at once, even before he is supposed to be qualified.

Most schools will employ as teacher an M.A. who is promising— that is, who is likely to become a Ph.D. This is an act of faith, good for only a limited period. There will be neither advancement nor increase of salary unless the Big League letters are secured. If the young teacher fails to grasp the situation in the large and shows a tendency to be content with his classwork and with his expanding family, the head of the school will tell him plainly that a permanent condition of M.A.-hood is irreconcilable with the intellectual life, and only up-and-coming intellectuals are wanted on the faculty.

If as I assume the M.A. is married, his wife will see the point even sooner than he. If the Ph.D. were only a door to knowledge it might be postponed a while longer, but if it is the condition which must precede a larger salary or a call elsewhere, then husband had better sit up nights and stretch his brain a little. If there is a child, the wife may advocate study for the doctorate even before the school head begins to threaten. One infant in the family makes the degree highly desirable, two make it obligatory. Since Father will try to earn his letters while he continues to earn a salary, the children may be grown up before he's a Doctor, and they will share their mother's interest in Father's studies, and more particularly, in his marks. The married M.A. candidate is subjected to such domestic backseat driving as, if it could be foreseen, would invest celibacy with unsuspected charm. By the time Father reaches his Ph.D. examination he is nervous, but the examiners make allowance for nervousness, and in a few minutes his eldest child will run home to his wife, who is changing the youngest, with the blessed news, "It's all right, Mama! Papa has passed!"

But we anticipate. It will be remembered that five years are consumed in obtaining the Master's degree. Two more are needed for the doctorate, seven in all, exactly the time Jacob would have invested in Rachel if he hadn't slipped up and got Leah instead. The Ph.D. candidate too sometimes has to go back and begin again, but if he's lucky he can hope for the letters in seven years. The sixth year is spent in running down a thesis subject and nibbling at it. In the seventh year the nibbling is completed and the thesis written.

The doctoral thesis is no more likely to be a thesis than the Doctor of Philosophy is likely to be a doctor or a philosopher. In the examination for the medieval doctorate the candidate did indeed take up an intellectual position and defend it against all comers, but we moderns avoid general propositions, as though they were bad for the brain. A Doctor's thesis today is simply an essay or a booklet which hopes to indicate that the author knows a good deal about some subject of which other teachers know nothing. Subjects which have the double usefulness of demonstrating ignorance as well as knowledge, were long ago exhausted. The sixth year, we said, was spent in running down something which earlier degree-hunters missed. But the word "running" might mislead. The candidate joins a seminar and sits down. Seminars are conducted by elderly or rapidly drying professors of wide reading, of great ingenuity, and of kind disposition, but with an eccentric notion of social responsibility, who furnish thesis subjects to the empty-headed.

We might suppose, if we didn't know better, that even a young scholar would be able to pick out some section on the frontier of his subject, if not a few miles than at least a few inches, which need exploring. But the candidate will probably drop into the seminar-giver's office. The seminar-giver will pretend he doesn't know what the candidate is there for. "Professor," blurts the candidate, "I have for some months been occupied or possessed by a subject which refuses to articulate itself." If the professor happens to be tired and irritable he may ask cruelly just what the inarticulate subject is. If he is in a softer mood, he'll say that in his experience when one subject refuses to be expressed, it's well to try another. "Naturally," comes back the candidate wriggling into position, "I have a list of things demanding treatment, but they all cover too much ground. I prefer to isolate a small question, and exhaust it." "The very spirit of scholarship," exclaims the professor, highly gratified, knowing that it will be his task to superintend the treatment of the important question. "I find that the most satisfactory theses are compact."

The candidate may take heart from the agreement between himself and the professor, but he still doesn't know what subject they are agreeing about. "Perhaps you might attend my seminar," suggests the guileless professor. "It meets at ten in the morning, twice a week. At every session there are reports and discussions, and a consequent germination and discharge of ideas which might be helpful. At least you will observe the present tendency of research. Several other members of the seminar are working in the same field with you." Though the candidate still doesn't know what his field is, he joins the seminar, exposes himself to promptings and broad hints twice a week, and in no time at all is equipped with a thesis subject.

After that he has nothing to fear. He reads his thesis to the seminar piece by piece as he writes it, and he accepts the professor's criticisms, every one of them. When the work is complete, the department accepts it, which ought to surprise nobody, seeing that a member of the department chose the subject and practically wrote the thing, the candidate acting merely as secretary and research assistant. And at the final examination the same professor, in the presence of his colleagues, takes the candidate over the hurdles, asking his reason for offering a thesis on this particular subject, and probing into the methods of search and research by which he obtained such interesting results. The other professors then reward themselves for listening by asking the candidate what he knows besides what went into the thesis, and here the candidate is unlikely to shine, but it is just as well, since his embarrassment makes his examiners genial if not magnanimous, and they soon vote to pass him.

Perhaps we're ahead of our story again. There's more to say about those thesis subjects. Don't forget that the Ph.D. and all the steps that lead up to it are supposed to have something to do with excellence in teaching. The thesis subject, then, should have some bearing on the subject the Doctor of Philosophy will teach, and on the way he will teach it.

In the sciences the thesis subjects are better than in literature, history and philosophy, or if they are not really better at least their weakness is less obvious to the layman. A Ph.D. in chemistry who has investigated any problem whatever is likely to know quite a bit about chemistry, enough to teach an elementary class anyway, but a doctorate in English does not necessarily imply an interest in literature nor knowledge of it. It may be that the best Ph.D. subjects in literature have already been worked to death. The English thesis more often than not is a biography of some author so insignificant that no one ever before was moved to write about him. In the first half of the thesis are assembled the facts known or guessable about this all-but-forgotten ghost. In the second half of the book the candidate, following hints from the professor in the seminar, examines critically the dull verse or prose which the ghost put forth while flesh covered his bones. The cadaver can be galvanized long enough for Ph.D. purposes but no longer, and cases have occurred where the student, forgetting the frailty of what he worked on, indulged in a vigorous sneeze, whereupon his subject lost its form and collapsed into a fine powder.

Serious scholars now prefer a subject which will show signs of life longer than is strictly necessary, several months or even a year beyond the granting of the degree and the publication of the thesis. Surprising vitality is found in certain tough and wiry questions which follow literary investigation without becoming a part of it. For example— What was the difference between the way Coleridge took his opium and the way De Quincey took his? Was there a difference in the quality of what they consumed? Is there here an explanation of the superiority of Coleridge's writing? A thrifty professor can spread this idea over several students and they all can pull a thesis out of it, one maintaining that Coleridge was a better writer than De Quincey, another that De Quincey was better than Coleridge, still another insisting that there's no difference between them.

Was Milton as blind as he thought? Would a skillful operation have restored his sight? Would such a recovery have been a benefit to English poetry? Similarly, what was the effect of Shelley's diet upon his writing? Should he have taken his friend Peacock's advice —one mutton chop well peppered for lunch or dinner? These subjects are all in the current fashion. I give them only by way of illustration, and perhaps I should warn Ph.D. candidates that some of them have already been used.

If books on such subjects qualify students for the Doctor's degree, we might as well ask whether the degree should any longer qualify them to teach. Some preliminary discipline there must be, but hardly the same discipline for those who would teach the humanities as for those who teach science. It is in the nature of science that its frontiers are constantly advancing and expanding. The young scientist is trained to make discoveries and report them, with the expectation that he will continue his discoveries and his reports all his life. He may have a literary gift, but usually he does very well without it, since his reports are made to other scientists, and his subject is probably dealt with most conveniently in mathematical symbols and equations rather than in words.

Why should the student of chemistry and the student of literature both write Ph.D. theses, to demonstrate their competence in their subject? If the purpose of the thesis were to show that the future teacher of literature knew how to produce it, then the present discipline might for its purpose at least be respected. But even so it is known that the ability to write can be demonstrated in a short piece, and command of the art is acquired more surely by the habitual composition of essays than by the production of a book on one unique occasion. If that single book is a thesis, it won't be literature, as a properly trained teacher of literature should be the first to know. The true writer, like any other artist, addresses a wide audience, and the more broadly human his appeal, the better writer he will be. If he is sincere a large percentage of his subject matter is personal to himself, but his art is to make it seem personal to each of many readers. A Ph.D. thesis may be distinguished from literature by these two marks, that the author has no readers in mind, or none besides the examining professors, and he expects and hopes never to write a thesis again.

There have been successful teachers of history who were not historians, and inspiring teachers of literature who were not writers. Why should they be detained from their life work by a wretched thesis? I hold the opinion that even such good teachers as these would impress their students more deeply and influence society more widely if they could write as well as talk. All teachers should learn early how to write, especially if writing is precisely what they are to teach. Practical experience as a writer is valuable if not essential for the teacher of history as well as for the teacher of literature. If you have written a history or a novel, you will know the difficulties and the pitfalls and you'll be better equipped to tell a good book from a bad one.

After all, the teacher of literature should know something about books, and he should know how to teach. A discipline which prepared him in these two directions would be a vast improvement on the seven-year process which ends dubiously in a Ph.D. thesis. Whatever the subject of his thesis, his students will not wish him to teach it to them; they will want from him presumably instruction which increases their understanding and appreciation of great books. He must therefore have first of all an acquaintance with the literature not of one country alone but of every important country, East and West. To know the great books of the world is work for a lifetime, but a lover of books will begin his reading early, and his university discipline should be merely a concentration and speeding up of a habit already formed. He will continue to read even after he has begun to teach, and his teaching might as well begin as soon as he has a fair grasp of his immense subject, at least in outline, and as soon as his enthusiasm for books in general is tempered with some discrimination.

But teaching is an art, and professors should have some training in it. I make this recommendation out of pity for college classes. We wouldn't think of turning loose an untrained teacher on the children in the kindergarten, but anyone with a Doctor's degree is supposed to be good enough for freshmen and sophomores. As a matter of fact, the college professor is not expected to teach; sometimes he does, but he is paid only to lecture. Even for lecturing he has had no training, but our faith is that God, having provided lungs and vocal organs, will send inspiration also.

A sane education for teachers of literature, and perhaps for all teachers in the humanities, could be imparted within a total period of six years; for certain individuals, within a shorter time. Members of the freshman class who show a love of books and an aptitude for thoughtful study, should be encouraged and guided in their reading; at the end of four years they can show a wider knowledge of books than we now dare expect from the average M.A. One more year of intense reading will give them an intimate acquaintance with the masterpieces in the whole field of literature. And during these five years they can learn to write.

The sixth year should be spent in teaching, under the observation and direction of the professors who have trained them. It would be only fair for the university which expects to wish them on other places, to try them out first on its own premises.

At the end of six years another diploma might be given to those who have convinced both their professors and their students that they can teach. But the diploma will probably not be needed. A good teacher is so rare that the rumor of him spreads with the speed of scandal.

CHAPTER XIV

Phi Beta Kappa

1

11 Quincy Street, Cambridge.

Professor John Erskine—

Dear Sir, As Chairman of The Literary Committee of the Harvard Phi B K Society, I have the pleasure of informing you that you have been unanimously chosen our Poet for our annual meeting on Monday, June 20, at noon.

The exercises, consisting of an Oration and Poem, are held in Sanders Theatre before an audience of somewhat more than 500, made up of members of the Society and their invited friends. I have no need to explain to you the special dignity of the occasion. You undoubtedly know the eminence of those who customarily serve us.

.   .   .   .   .   .

You will receive a hearty welcome, and I shall find a special pleasure in making the acquaintance of one whom I have long known.

Very truly yours,

G. H. PALMER

November 2, 1920.

I did indeed recognize the compliment contained in this invitation, and I knew more about the extraordinary person who addressed the letter to me than he perhaps realized. Not that it would have made the slightest difference to him.

Professor George Herbert Palmer was nearly seventy-nine years old on the second of November, 1920, and he continued in health and vigor until his death at the age of ninety-one. Since 1870 he had taught at Harvard, first as a tutor in Greek, afterward as a modest but very important member of the Philosophy department. Since he considered himself a teacher of philosophy rather than a creative thinker, the academic world took him at his own valuation, and ranked him somewhat below his colleagues in the brilliant Harvard group, William James, Josiah Royce, Hugo Münsterberg and George Santayana. But Palmer had a large part in assembling these strong but divergent characters, and a still larger part in holding them together, to work as a team. Now Santayana had retired to Europe, where to this day he continues to make his career out of being a refugee. James died in 1910, Royce and Münsterberg in 1916. Palmer retired in 1913, but continued to live in the Quincy Street house, himself a Harvard institution, self-contained and self-sustaining.

When Woodberry came to Harvard in the class of 1876, he attracted the kindly interest of Professor Palmer, who invited him to occupy a room in the Quincy Street home. Since Woodberry was a poor boy, this hospitality was a godsend. Now I looked forward to meeting a friend and benefactor of the greatest of all my teachers.

I was conscious also of the special glamour which Harvard has bequeathed to the ceremonies with which American colleges keep the anniversary of their unique honor society, membership in which is the reward of undergraduate scholarship. If we have learned to expect some extraordinary pronouncement of youth and idealism at the annual meetings of Phi Beta Kappa, the reasons are two; in 1782 the Harvard Chapter started the custom of celebrating the day with exercises consisting of an oration and an original poem; and on August 31, 1837, the orator of the day, Ralph Waldo Emerson, took for his subject "The American Scholar," and delivered what we still revere as the Declaration of our Intellectual Independence.

Professor Palmer must have heard frequent reminders of what Emerson said, and of the mixed emotions with which the brave message had been received. Perhaps the keynote of the famous speech would have been a little too bold for him, as it was for some of Emerson's audience. Well enough to say that the New World should withdraw from under the dead hand of the Old, but why suggest that the New World in time would have a dead hand of its own? *The Late George Apley* had not yet been thought of.

I reached 11 Quincy Street on the afternoon of June 19. Professor Palmer would be absent from the Phi Beta Kappa exercises the next day. Wellesley College was remembering its distinguished President, Alice Freeman, who had been his second wife, and he wished to hear the tributes in her honor. To compensate for his absence from the Harvard ceremonies I was to have his undivided attention at dinner and through an evening of talk.

The accounts that Woodberry and others had given, prepared me for my first meeting with this genial man, quiet-seeming but never silent for long. When Woodberry started on his teaching career in Nebraska, he doubted if he could lecture for fifty minutes.

"You can do it for sixty, if necessary," Professor Palmer assured him. "Any man can talk longer than that on any subject."

I spoke of his rare fortune in having such colleagues as James and the others. "Rare indeed," he agreed. "When James was writing his *Varieties of Religious Experience,* he would send me two or three short letters a day, notes of ideas he wished to share. He kept that up for two or three years!"

"The letters must be an almost complete record of his daily thoughts."

"They were."

I noticed the shift of tense. "Did you ever publish them?"

For a moment he was puzzled. "The letters? Certainly not! They were personal communications—not for publication."

"But some day, Professor Palmer—surely you will share with scholars in your subject a legacy so interesting—"

I thought his smile was tolerant of my crudeness. "My dear fellow, those letters were all burned, as fast as I received them. I never keep a letter after it is answered. With one exception! James wrote me his opinion of Santayana's *Interpretations of Poetry and Religion,* and since it was a long letter, and to save himself the trouble of writing it twice, he asked me to hand on my copy. Later when Henry James was making his edition of his father's *Letters,* Santayana gave him everything he had, including the one letter to me."

I asked Professor Palmer his opinion of George Santayana, whom at that time I admired fanatically. "Do you mean personally or philosophically? We got on very well. His superiority to the human race was rather amusing. As to the value of his philosophizing, James hit it off in that letter. It was like Santayana to enjoy the castigation from James, and to preserve it for posterity."

At the first opportunity I looked up the letter, dated April 2, 1900: "I now understand Santayana, the man. I never understood him before. But what a perfection of rottenness in a philosophy! I don't think I ever knew the anti-realistic view to be propounded with so impudently superior an air. It is refreshing to see a representative of moribund Latinity rise up and administer such reproof to us barbarians in the hour of our triumph."

I enjoyed comparing James on Santayana with Santayana on William James, in *Character and Opinion in the United States:* "His father was one of those somewhat obscure sages whom early America produced: mystics of independent mind, hermits in the desert of business, and heretics in the churches. They were intense individualists, full of veneration for the free souls of their children, and convinced that every one should paddle his own canoe, especially on the high seas. . . . On points of art or medicine he retained a professional touch and an unconscious ease which he hardly acquired in metaphysics. I suspect he had heartily admired some of his masters in those other subjects, but had never seen a philosopher whom he would have cared to resemble."

I knew already some of the impish side of Santayana's character. When he left Harvard he presented to the University Library the autographed copies of books written by his colleagues. During the war a member of the Library staff told me he cut the pages of these gift books before exposing them on the shelves. Santayana had not read one of them.

What Santayana thought of my elderly host, I had no idea as I listened to Professor Palmer in his study that mild June evening. But in *Persons and Places,* the first instalment of Santayana's autobiography, I found this portrait, in 1944, when Palmer had been in his grave more than ten years. It was really quite perfect. None of these professors had really thought very highly of the others, but their manners were of the best, and they were, in their various ways, precise truth-tellers, masters of the qualified phrase. I was grateful that I had known Woodberry, a less brittle Harvard product.

"Professor Palmer," says Santayana,* "practised all the smooth rhetorical arts of a liberal parson or headmaster; he conciliated opponents, plotted (always legally) with friends, and if things went against him, still smiled victoriously and seemed to be on the crest of the wave. He was the professor of ethics. His lectures were beautifully prepared, and exactly the same year after year. He had been professor of Greek also, and made anodyne translations from Homer and Sophocles in 'rhythmic' and sleepy prose. In his courses on English moralists he brought out his selected authors in dialectical order; each successive view appeared fresh and plausible, but not sensational. They came in a subtle crescendo, everything good, and everything a little better than what went before, so that at the end you ought to have found yourself in the seventh heaven. Yet we, or at least I, didn't find ourselves there. I felt myself cheated.

* From *Persons and Places* by George Santayana. New York. Charles Scribner's Sons, 1944.

The method was Hegelian adapted to a Sunday School; all roses
without thorns. . . . 'Purring pussy Palmer,' my sporting friend
'Swelly' Bangs used to call him. Yet Palmer was a benign influence.
The crude, half-educated, conscientious, ambitious young men who
wished to study ethics gained subtler and more elastic notions of
what was good than they had ever dreamt of: and their notions of
what was bad became correspondingly discriminating and fair.
Palmer was like a father confessor, never shocked at sin, never
despairing of sinners. There must be a little of everything in the
Lord's vineyard. Palmer was a fountain of sweet reasonableness.
That his methods were sophistical and his conclusions lame didn't
really matter. It was not a question of discovering or deciding anything final: the point was to become more cultivated and more
intelligent."

I made a feeble attempt to draw out Palmer on the subject of
Woodberry, but soon ˙gave it up. The old Professor was so far
advanced in age that a pupil from nearly half a century ago never
grew up. He spoke of my teacher as the young man he had taken
into his house; he remembered him as very promising, likely to go
far. He said it so gently that I wondered if he forgot the years, or
whether he imitated Shakspere's ironic habit, and referred to the
journey beyond time which most of his colleagues had taken, and
Woodberry and he would soon take.

Then he suggested that my trip from New York might have tired
me, and we parted for the night.

Next morning, shortly after breakfast, a car came to carry Professor Palmer to the Wellesley ceremonies. Somewhat later I joined
the Phi Beta Kappa members who were assembling in the Yard.

2

The orator of the day was to be Ralph Adams Cram, then at the
height of his fame as a master of Gothic architecture. Thanks to
him there was a rising Gothic cult in the Eastern states, particularly

in New England. Putnam Brinley, one of his devoted admirers, had preached to me the advantages of Gothic architecture while we were trying to keep clear of the mud at Sommedieue.

I was eager to meet Mr. Cram and to hear him. No one doubted that he would devote his Phi Beta Kappa address to his favorite theme. It was amusing to think that the Harvard Chapter, before whom, or their predecessors, Emerson had read "The American Scholar," would now hear a call, not to live in their own day and to express themselves, but to worship at long-neglected shrines, and to revive in the United States of America, especially at Cambridge, Massachusetts, the spirit of the Middle Ages. In order to avoid a jarring note of modernity, I brought, as my contribution to the program, a paraphrase of the story of Sir Graelent, as told in medieval legend.

I found Mr. Cram with the other assembled guests. After a newspaper reporter photographed us together I had some moments of delightful talk with him. Though he would read his address, he had thought so much about it that the ideas spilled themselves now in casual remarks. The earnestness of his Gothic convictions and their unexpected range amazed me. I began to think he was only by accident an architect; his primary interest was philosophy; he wished to be a prophet of a wiser and happier society, and the key to his millennium was, he believed, the complete recovery of the Middle Ages, a return to society as it existed in the thirteenth century, a reform of industry, of labor, of capital, of education—so that if a good scholastic should happen to cross the Harvard Yard some bright morning, he could easily imagine himself in the fields of Paris on the Left Bank of the Seine.

Mr. Cram touched on this dream of his in swift and eloquent phrases. There was no opportunity just then to develop his ideas; he was a popular figure, and one distinguished Harvard personage after another came up and claimed his attention.

At the proper moment a little procession was formed, the two speakers with their escorts. The other members of Phi Beta Kappa, past and present, took their places in two long rows, between which we walked to Sanders Theatre, the circular hall where Harvard holds its Commencements and other ceremonies. The speakers and their escorts mounted the platform, the two long rows of distinguished Phi Beta Kappas took their seats in the body of the little theatre, the invited guests were ranged in the galleries.

Nothing that was said there that morning impressed me so much as the quality of the men who were gathered there to listen. A better sampling of New England culture would have been difficult to assemble—well-known judges and other members of the Bar, writers whose names had been known in the land for a quarter-century, the Librarian of Congress, and others closely related to the life of the nation and to scholarship. My friend Professor Daly greeted me with his warm handgrasp and a word of our educational work together in France, Professor Charles Grandgent, the Dante scholar, warm-hearted friend and poetry lover, had a comprehensive welcome for us, as though a Phi Beta Kappa poem and the oration were just what he had been living to hear.

Mr. Cram's speech was doubly remarkable after the preliminary glimpses of it I had enjoyed. Very thoroughly he expanded the framework indicated by what had seemed random remarks. He was speaking at the end of the First World War, when all thoughtful people felt something of the lack of confidence in the future which troubles us even more deeply today. Cram laid down the theory in no uncertain tones that to re-establish itself in the moral world society must go back to the thirteenth century and reorganize every aspect of its life on models provided by the ages of faith. The workman must love his work and believe in its importance; the merchant must be proud of his ministrations to other men, and must feel his obligation to render true service and purvey honest goods; the lawyer and the scholar must be animated by the love of justice and of truth. If all work had for its motive a passionate love of mankind, a love of service, a love of the materials which are employed in serviceable ways, then men would have the right kinds of satisfaction in their work, the proper sense of the goodness of life, and a true appreciation of beauty.

In detail the speaker described the change which would come over business and the learned professions if the medieval philosophy should be restored. Practically all of his hearers had been taught to admire the advances of the modern world which came in with the Renaissance. We found ourselves listening to an attack on everything which we considered progress. As he warmed toward his climax, Mr. Cram told us that there had been no progress, but rather a steady deterioration throughout the last five hundred years. Civilization had slipped down the hill since Dante walked the streets of Florence or climbed inhospitable stairways in Ravenna. The central point of the address was the striking announcement that the moment in history when all the arts met in the condition of their highest perfection occurred during the celebration of High Mass in the thirteenth century. I have not looked at the text of his address since I heard his delivery of it; perhaps he located the celebration of High Mass in some particular cathedral. Perhaps he said that all the arts met in their highest perfection during the celebration of High Mass at Chartres in the thirteenth century.

However he may have made his point, I was busy watching the faces of his audience as he made it. On the seats in the theatre below him sat the distinguished Phi Beta Kappas, product of the old Congregational or Unitarian puritanism. Whatever vestige of theology still clung to them, they practiced a religion of courteous self-control—what emotional barbarians like myself from New York would recognize as Bostonian religion. I can see those faces now, turned up to Ralph Cram with the closest of polite and chilly attention. He might just as well have been speaking about Dr. Einstein's theory, or the proper use of the atomic bomb, or desirable changes in masculine costume for hot weather. I thought of the benefits which Santayana had ascribed to Professor Palmer's years of teaching. Here was an illustration of what happened to a man when he came under the benign influence, and was watered by the fountain of sweet reasonableness. "It was not a question of discovering or deciding anything final: the point was to become more cultivated and more intelligent."

I may seem to attach undue significance to this Phi Beta Kappa meeting. It stands out in my memory as a gracious and dignified occasion in which I was proud to have a part. I enjoyed kind hospitality, and I was stirred by the memories of a great university. But I was asking myself, if this is the upshot of scholarship and educational effort, then what is the value of education and scholarship? Is the total result a loss of enthusiasm or ardor or faith for the world in which we must live, and a somewhat nostalgic respect for an age that is past beyond recall? Would not a return to faith show itself now in terms of modern life, just as in the Middle Ages it showed itself in the life of those days? If Mr. Cram had said that the arts *ought* to meet in their greatest perfection during a celebration of High Mass, his doctrine would have been understandable, but I did not gather that he was inviting us to go to High Mass today; he was making us wish we could attend Mass in the thirteenth century. To me the suggestion was ridiculous, just as Gothic buildings in American colleges or at West Point seem anachronistic and in absurd contrast to American life. If education is not to help us to live wisely in the day to which we belong, then education, I fear, is a mischievous enterprise. The tragedy of European culture is the extent to which it tangles itself inextricably with the past. By way of contrast, the hope of American culture is its opportunity to get free of the past, and to establish, as Emerson said, a direct relation with Nature, or if you please, with God.

But such ideas as these I knew at the time were too serious for the occasion. As the audience dispersed after the ceremony some delightful gentleman, doing full credit to the education in which he had been trained, showed me the right comment to make, with the proper degree of self-control and enlightenment, and with the minimum extravagance of feeling. I heard behind me in well-bred tones, "Cram was in form this morning, was he not?"

CHAPTER XV

Last Talks with Woodberry

AFTER I resumed my teaching at Columbia, in the autumn of
1919, I had a long talk with Woodberry on two occasions,
one provided by Professor A. V. Williams Jackson, the other con-
trived by myself. These were not my last glimpses of my old
teacher, but I remember them as my last opportunities to talk with
him intimately and at length.

At the University one morning Professor Jackson told me that
Woodberry was coming to New York, and had expressed the wish
to see me and hear about the Beaune experiences. On one of the
evenings of his stay the Jacksons were going to the theatre and
would leave him at home to entertain me. I grasped the opportunity.

Woodberry was waiting in the Jackson library, where the great
Persian scholar had left some refreshments for us on the table in
case we talked our throats dry. Woodberry, descendant of New
England sea captains, was not a teetotaler, but Jackson was—or at
least he had a sincere preference for soft rather than hard drinks.
I doubt if he ever ventured further than a mug of beer at our undergraduate King's Crown meetings. As I came into the library that
evening and saw the gingerale bottles, I thought for how many years
I had witnessed this and other differences of taste between the de-

voted friends—differences which counted for nothing between them, though Woodberry had no natural admiration for men who could warm their hearts on a glass of water. We talked for a while about the war and about the University at Beaune. Though Woodberry was interested and asked keen questions, it seemed to me that his thoughts were ahead of my story. Lolling back in his easy chair, enjoying his cigar, as in our after-lunch talks long before in my Amherst study, he was turning over in his mind questions I hadn't yet touched. When there was no more to say about Beaune he began to cross-examine me.

"Are you glad to be back at your teaching?"

I told him I was.

"They say you've been called to more than one university as president."

I said the rumor was correct.

"Why did you decline?"

"Because I would rather teach and write."

The answer seemed not to satisfy him, not entirely; I restated my reasons.

"If I hadn't guessed it before, Beaune would have taught me I wasn't born to be an officeholder."

He smiled, plainly relieved. "You want to be a free man."

"I want to teach and write," I insisted. "A college president must provide ways and means for others to teach and write, but he himself misses all the fun, though perhaps he might teach better than any of his faculty."

Woodberry laughed silently. "Well, if you've learned some first principles, I'm not surprised; you have crossed the ocean, and you have seen a war."

He began to ask about my students. "Do any of them write? Are there poets among them?"

I described my group of ambitious poets and fiction writers, adding a word about the books they knew. "Few of them have English or American literature in their background. Their acquaintance with great Anglo-Saxon writers probably began in school."

"But do they know other writers?"

I said they did—Russian writers, Central European writers.

"Then there's nothing to worry about," said Woodberry. "One culture takes the place of another. It has always been so, it will always be. Don't worry so long as they do read and do create."

Gradually our talk reverted to old days at Columbia, not because I wished to dwell on the past, but because he, revisiting the neighborhood where his great work had been done, wanted to speak of his Columbia triumphs and of his Columbia troubles. Once or twice he tried to rouse himself from this mood. We opened Professor Jackson's innocent bottles, which went very well with the delicious cake and the cool fruit on the hospitable tray. But after a few cheerful sallies, Woodberry would retreat again into the shadow.

When the Jacksons returned at midnight, I went away a little saddened.

Because this meeting ended on a note of age and discouragement, I resolved to see Woodberry again and gather a different kind of memory. Often though he had spoken of his home in Beverly, I had never seen it. There, if anywhere, he would be at his best. In October, 1921, I wrote him that an errand would take me to Boston, and I wanted at the same time to drop in on him at Beverly. I had no Boston errand, but if he knew I was making the trip entirely on his account, he might not take my visit so casually as I hoped he would.

He wrote back that Saturday, November 5, would be a convenient day for him. "I think your best train will be at 10:05 from Boston, reaching Beverly at 11:00. You will stay to lunch; and there are trains nearly every hour from Beverly to Boston up to the evening. We can have a long day of talk. I will come down to meet you, if you say you will come then; and anyway, the walk up is short, and there are always cabs at the station.

"What a brief note! but there's welcome in it aplenty. All our little family are well, and we shall be glad to have you *en famille,* though there will be nothing French about the cuisine."

He was waiting for me at the station in a sharp, chilly wind, with his heavy coat wrapped close around him, and his soft hat nearly blown off his head. In spite of the weather he proposed a walk to the woods and the shore which he had loved since boyhood, and where he still took the small amount of exercise he thought necessary for health.

"Or perhaps you would rather come to the house first and warm up."

I chose an immediate walk, being quite sure his energy would be spent in a few minutes. Before we had gone a mile, he declared that the weather was unpleasant, and we might as well enjoy his study fire. His Beverly home was an old house, built rather low and seeming smaller than it was. Under this roof had lived his paternal ancestors for five generations, a succession of sea captains from father to son. Woodberry, having left the sea for poetry, liked to say they were the same thing. His study, a large room in the front of the house, had perhaps been the kitchen in the eighteenth or seventeenth century. The large fireplace looked as though it had once contained an oven on each side. In this room Woodberry had been born. Now there was little except the fireplace to suggest the ancient kitchen, and nothing to recall a bedroom. The ceiling was low, the walls were lined with books.

Beyond the study the house rambled into a dining room with a modern kitchen, and beyond that a typical New England woodshed, spacious and enclosed. There was a second story containing the bedrooms, which must have been very small. The staircase and the hallways were lined with books, hundreds of them. No doubt the bedrooms contained the overflow of the immense library. Not all of the books had been of Woodberry's own collecting; his people, I believe, had always been readers, and I noticed on the shelves some old bindings.

Living with Woodberry at the time were his sister and two brothers, all approximately of his own age, in the early sixties. The sister had prepared an excellent meal for us, which I have forgotten in detail except that there was a thick steak superbly cooked. Woodberry, at the head of the table, did the carving, and I stored away for further reflection the picture of him in this domestic, even patriarchal, attitude. He was happy among his people, presiding over the hospitality of the old house; he also appreciated the steak, which, he remarked, was of a quality he had rarely met since boyhood. His sister asked whether the walk might not have given him an appetite, but he insisted that the steak was notable in its own right. Knowing how brief and easy the walk had been, I agreed with him.

After lunch he lighted his customary cigar, put a fresh log on the study fire, and settled down in a comfortable-looking but somewhat battered chair, leaving to me a younger and possibly more dependable seat. We were ready for a long talk which had many high points. Three of them I recall vividly.

In his essay on Taormina he had mentioned the paper-bound volumes of local legend or history which the Keeper of the communal library gave him. Sitting now among his books I asked if he still had these Taorminian treasures, the inspiration of his beautiful essay. He thought he had them—couldn't lay his hand on them—started to search the house. Having caught up with them at last, dust-covered on a shelf upstairs, he brought them down triumphantly, settled again into his seat by the fire, and studied them with me.

In the front pages he had drawn for his own use, years before, maps of the footpaths around Taormina. He had forgotten them, and the rediscovery gave him intense pleasure. Fingering through the time-colored pages he would pause from moment to moment for a happy word of comment or explanation. I thought there was a special light in his face as he relived the Italian days which fill his writings.

Early in 1921 I read the letters of William James, published the year before, and now Woodberry's talk of Taormina reminded me of the philosopher's comment on *The Heart of Man,* in which the essay on Taormina appeared. But as James made clear, he read only the second and third chapters; so far as I know he may never have glanced at the account of Taormina.

His comment, for what it is worth, occurs in a letter to Mrs. Henry Whitman, dated June 7, 1899.

"A word about Woodberry's book. I didn't know him to be that kind of a creature at all. The essays are grave and noble in the extreme. I hail another American author. They can't be popular, and for cause. The respect of him for the Queen's English, the classic leisureliness and explicitness, which give so rare a dignity to his style, also take from it that which our generation seems to need, the sudden word, the unmeditated transition, the flash of perception that makes reasonings unnecessary. Poor Woodberry, so high, so true, so good, so original in his total make-up, and yet so unoriginal if you take him spot-wise—and therefore so ineffective. His paper on Democracy is very fine indeed, though somewhat too abstract. I haven't yet read the first and last essays in the book, which I shall buy and keep, and even send a word of gratulation to the author for it."

I asked Woodberry if he had read this passage in James. He recalled it immediately.

"Did he send you the 'word of gratulation'?"

Smiling quietly, Woodberry got up, went to a small letter file, took out a folder, and gave me James's note, written the same day as the letter to Mrs. Whitman. It contained all the praise and none of the strictures, all the "high, true, good, original in his total make-up," not a hint of the "so unoriginal if you take him spot-wise."

I handed back the twenty-year-old page. I was ready, and am now, to admit the truth in James's acute verdict on Woodberry's leisurely style, but I didn't admire the frank criticism behind his back, and the apparently whole-hearted praise to his face. I must have said something of the kind, for Woodberry laughed.

"I ought not to have kept that letter. Perhaps all letters should be destroyed, certainly those from women, and I dare say those from men too. One of my old letters embarrassed me in Boston the other day. When the Authors Club was organized, years ago, they asked me to join and I said I would on three conditions; first that there should be a clubhouse, and no meetings should be held in a private home, second, that the first president should be Thomas Bailey Aldrich, and third, that no women should be admitted to the Club except in a condition of servitude."

He glanced up, to be sure I understood. "I meant, of course, scrubwomen."

"But nowadays the women writers can join, and most of them do. The Club gave a reception in my honor recently. Very kind of them. As soon as I went in, one of those women took me by the arm and led me across the room to a framed manuscript. They had framed that old letter of mine. It was a horrid experience."

On the desk near the window lay a well-printed pamphlet. Woodberry got it and drew his chair close to mine, so he could read the thing into my ear. "You must hear this. It says what I have always said. It will be good for you."

It was an address on Walt Whitman which Lord Charnwood had delivered before the British Academy. Woodberry never liked Walt; I always did. Lord Charnwood thought Walt was crude, not at all in good taste, not a gentleman.

At the end of the afternoon, Woodberry walked to the station with me. I had been in his house all day, and had received warm hospitality. Afterward I noticed that he had not once, in that ancestral spot, mentioned his father or his mother.

The closing chapter of *The Heart of Man*, the account of a conversation about religion, always bothered me. Other readers may have found the philosophical concept somewhat vague, but I was perplexed by statements of fact. The chapter is called "The Ride."

The incident is from Woodberry's western days, while he was
teaching at the University of Nebraska, from 1877 to 1878 or from
1880 to 1882. He and his friend, Eugene Montgomery, to whose
memory *The Heart of Man* is dedicated, exchanged their thoughts
about religion while driving a pair of ponies across the prairie.

Those ponies troubled me. They were wild one day, quite tame
and docile before the following dawn. Woodberry's description of
the animals in their wild state was so fine that I wanted the rest of
the story to be true.

"It was the frontier of our western border. A herd of Texas ponies
were to be immediately on sale, and I went to see them—wild
animals, beautiful in their wildness, who had never known bit or
spur; they were lariated and thrown down, as the buyers picked
them out, and then led and pulled away to man's life. It was a
typical scene: the pen, the hundred ponies bunched together and
startled with the new surroundings, the cowboys whose resolute
habit sat on them like cotillion grace—athletes in the grain—with
the gray close garb for use, the cigarette like a slow spark under the
sombrero, the belted revolver, the lasso hung loose-coiled in the
hand, quiet, careless, confident, with the ease of the master of his
craft, now pulling down a pony without a struggle, and now showing strength and dexterity against frightened resistance; but the hour
sped on, and our spoil was two of these creatures, so attractive to
me at least that every moment my friend's eye was on me, and he
kept saying, 'They're wild, mind.' The next morning in the dark
dawn we had them in harness, and drove out, when the stars were
scarce gone from the sky, due north to the Bad Lands."

I asked Woodberry about the passage, after we were finished with
William James and his letter-writing, and with the misadventure at
the Boston Authors Club. "Are wild ponies broken to harness and
taught to obey the bit in a few hours? From page to page I expected your raw ponies to overturn the wagon, or to lash out and
kick it to pieces, but you merely say it was fortunate they were not

restive both at the same time. Their behavior was so smooth that you take out your notebook and read your friend pages from it."

He took my question in good humor, but he had no answer. "It is long ago," he said. "Perhaps the ponies had been driven before. Or perhaps it was as I said. I cannot remember. What stays with me is the scene, the prairie world, and what we said."

My own memory of the afternoon at Beverly may be less certain than I think, but I set down these cherished fragments of talk because like James's comments they round out Woodberry's character and perhaps define him as a writer. But he was primarily a teacher, and his genius operated always to open our eyes to the human experiences within our reach; that first of all, and afterward to direct us toward whatever in literature expressed those experiences. And he was willing that he himself should be, for his boys, one illustration among others of that reservoir of dreams and confusion from which by a miracle the clear visions of poets and artists are drawn.

CHAPTER XVI

Lecture Tour

1

TO SOME extent every American professor is a public lecturer. If he isn't, he'd like to be. Nothing holds him back, if he really knows how to make a speech. For one public lecture he is sometimes paid much more than he earns teaching his class for a month, in school or college. But in school the class must be attentive for the whole hour. If the public lecturer is not interesting, he may have the room to himself.

I suppose there will always be among teachers some who disapprove of human happiness, who will insist that any instruction which gives pleasure to the instructed, probably does more harm than good. The teacher who is popular with his students will hardly be so with his colleagues. And he who draws crowds to hear him whenever he mounts the public platform will be scorned by the learned and dull as an entertainer.

I am here offering an *apologia* for my life in education. My classes at Amherst and Columbia were large, and I liked them to be so. All my life I have been a public lecturer, and I'd rather speak to a sizable audience than to a diminutive one. I am conscious of no obligation to explain why I feel this way. Unless a teacher fears

that what he teaches is not worth hearing, why shouldn't he speak
to as many as possible?

The fact is that many professors speak badly, sometimes inaudi-
bly, almost always without even a pretense at anything which can
be called art. Most of them excuse themselves by protesting that it
is not their function to entertain. That self-righteous statement will
bear close study. If the teacher expresses himself clearly, and uses
his vocal cords correctly, his communications to his class will give
pleasure as well as instruction. To that extent he is an entertainer.
But altogether too many teachers strain their voices to the discomfort
of their audience as well as themselves.

A lecture is a performance; and an artistic performance must be
planned and carefully prepared. When Professor Gilbert Murray
years ago was reading at Columbia his lectures on the four stages
of Greek religion, we were delighted and somewhat amazed at the
natural emphasis of every phrase. Though he read from a manuscript, the musical inflections were dictated, it seemed, by his heart.
After one lecture Professor Cassius J. Keyser borrowed the script,
and found every page of it marked with expression signs—pauses,
diminuendos, crescendos. The apparent spontaneity of Professor
Murray's incomparable delivery resulted from thorough preparations.

Since I had begun life expecting to be a musician, a pianist, I
knew that any performance worth listening to is well prepared, and
I rehearsed my lectures even when I did not use notes. Several of
my former students, describing me and my habits years later, said
that I was at times a prima donna. The criticism I suppose was fair;
at times the careful planning may have showed through; I may
have fallen short of Professor Murray's apparent spontaniety. But
I regret only that I missed the effect I tried for; I am glad that I
aimed always at a performance, a work of art; I was quite willing
that it should be my critics who open their mouths and let Nature
gasp.

Before 1925 I had given public lectures, both here and abroad, but
I had never toured my own land. Most of my talks in America had

been given in New York. But early in 1927 Louis J. Alber, of Cleveland, brought me an invitation to tour the United States from coast to coast, lecturing seven times a week, if so booked, between February 6, 1928, and April 14, both dates inclusive.

I signed this contract on March 2, 1927. The tour the following year began not on February 6 but on February 4, and ended not on April 14 but on April 28.

I was curious about the lecture audiences because I had heard of their psychology, and I wanted to form my own opinion. If the reports of other lecturers were correct, these ladies and gentlemen —chiefly ladies—were not interested exclusively in education. To a certain extent, according to report, they wished entertainment, and in 1928 they attended a lecture by the author of a popular book for the purpose merely of spending an hour or so in his company—much as the motion picture audiences like to spend an evening with Clark Gable or with Errol Flynn. But other reports were more flattering to the national character. Lectures were given before college audiences or before women's clubs or in public forums where questions follow the talk, or in other lecture series organized by the community in the general hope of self-improvement. I had been told frequently by lecturers from abroad, chiefly from England, that though there were ridiculous aspects of this American passion for listening to novelists who probably had already said in their book all they had to say, yet perhaps a new and useful branch of education was here springing up in our soil.

The Alber agency advertised that I would speak on the sources from which I had drawn material for my three novels, or on the philosophy which in my opinion lay behind the stories—the moral obligation to be intelligent. If I should be asked to talk about the various legends which circulated in the ancient world about Helen of Troy before Homer wrote her up, the audience would get entertainment, I hoped. So, if I were asked to tell the earliest legends about Launcelot, Guinevere, and Galahad. I guessed correctly that there would be no requests to hear the earliest stories about Adam and Eve; every lecture committee would assume that their clients knew that material from their Bible reading. If, however, I were asked to speak on "The Moral Obligation to be Intelligent," the audience would get as thought-provoking a discourse as I could put together. Though they might not entirely agree with me, they would encounter, perhaps, a number of new ideas, and I might tell them much about medieval and modern thinkers which habitually had been overlooked.

I started on this lecture tour, then, for the pleasure of meeting the audiences. I hoped that each group would teach me something about the character of my own people, whom, if I continued to write novels, I must understand.

But I undertook the lectures also to make the acquaintance of my country geographically. I had never been West as far as the Mississippi River. I knew little of Canada. I had not yet seen the Caribbean or the Gulf of Mexico. During my war experiences in France, and after the war, at Beaune, I realized that I was ignorant of America.

Let me say here by way of parenthesis that public lecturing remains for me to this day a source of continuous education. My audiences have changed slightly; nowadays I am usually asked to address a convention of teachers in some state. If they ask me, it may be because they have never yet heard me. Certainly it is true that the less familiar I am with them and their region, the surer I am to accept their invitation. Merely from watching such audiences, from listening to other speakers on the program with me, and from studying the city or town where the convention is· held, I have learned most of what I know outside of books.

2

In 1928 my tour began in the East, in New York City, in Brooklyn, in Saratoga Springs; Taunton, Massachusetts; Amsterdam, New York; Waterbury, Connecticut; Danbury, Connecticut. All these places were familiar to me. Saratoga I associated with my mother's girlhood. In her time the young people of Lansingburg, where she lived, looked upon Saratoga as the most attractive of all resorts. After my return from France I bought an old farm in Wilton, Connecticut, and turned it into a summer home. From Wilton I frequently drove over to Danbury and Waterbury; in fact, I had already lectured in both places.

In the second chapter of the tour I spoke at Elmira; at Morgantown, West Virginia; at Toledo, Ohio; at Cleveland, Ohio; at Detroit, Michigan; and again at Cleveland, Ohio.

An itinerant lecturer is usually disposed to think that his agent books him by preference in zigzags rather than in straight lines, but the agent has a good excuse when a large city like Cleveland wishes to engage a speaker for two separate dates. In the third week of my tour I spoke twice in Pittsburgh, and on the evening between, at Altoona. Then the tour speeded up, and I began to cover territory in sizable leaps.

In the third week of the tour, just before I was getting into the Deep South, I was asked by one of my audiences to play the piano for them, at the end of my speech. There was an excellent instrument on the platform which perhaps provoked the invitation, or it may be that someone had put the piano there to make it harder for me to escape. Having a few pieces in my fingers at the time, I played for nearly half an hour with no thought of the trouble I was storing up. The news spread that I would play if asked. For the rest of the tour I found myself putting on an elaborate show, first the lecture, then the brief recital. Had I been able to sing and to dance I have no doubt the audience would have tried to find out how well I could do those things too.

3

It might be asked why my colleagues were willing to let me do all this. What was happening to my courses meanwhile? The answer is simple. The English department was not disposed to let me go off on this jaunt, but I had asked the President and the Trustees for a leave of absence, and they had granted it. My colleagues knew that if they tried to prevent this lecture tour, I would resign. The conflicting theories we held about education, had strained our academic relations. The older professors did not approve of teachers who could and did write books. In their opinion I had ended much of my usefulness by becoming a novelist. But they were glad when my lectures in the department brought a large income, which went into the department budget for them to use as they chose. Though they criticized a kind of teaching which attracted large numbers, they saw no inconsistency in exploiting me.

My largest course was in the Graduate School. It was open to candidates for the Master's degree. I have not refreshed my memory of the exact registration, but at the time I proposed to make the country-wide lecture tour, I believe I had 225 students in the course. Each student paid $30 each half-year. The course therefore earned the English department $6,750 a semester, or $13,500 annually. My salary for the year was $7,500.

In addition to this large lecture course for M.A. candidates, I gave an undergraduate course in Elizabethan literature, a course which involved real teaching. The students, some forty of them, made numerous reports over which I held frequent consultations. I also gave a writing course for some thirty carefully selected students. They wrote for me stories, poems, and plays, which we discussed in class and in private. Most of the boys in this class belonged to an informal group who once a fortnight spent an evening with me in my home, reading their pieces aloud and criticizing them at length. I loved this work, and I gladly would have added to the budget of the English department by continuing to give courses for which it might seem I was not paid. But I was unwilling indefinitely to put up with the benighted and repressive attitude of the men who controlled the department's policy. Perhaps the free hand the Army had given me in building up the school at Beaune had spoiled me. I could not be happy watching others make mistakes I had learned to avoid, nor would I admit their vested right to impose worn-out patterns on a new day. The unwillingness to call Stuart Sherman I continued to think a tragic error. I should always resist the doctrine that the end of our teaching should be to produce, not writers or creative spirits, but docile and stationary folk, who would remember what they had been told, and repeat it to their pupils, and never, never disturb the peace with a new idea.

Before my lecture tour began my associates on the Board of the Juilliard School of Music, then seeking a president, persuaded me without much difficulty to undertake the organization of what was as yet only a fascinating idea. Though the call was to administrative and executive duties, and though I preferred to teach, I accepted this, one of the most constructive tasks I ever had, not unlike the opportunity at Beaune. Columbia extended my leave of absence. The elder statesmen of the English department said goodbye to me cordially. Then, I suppose, they drew a long breath.

When I left Columbia for the Juilliard School, I did not determine to give up teaching. President Butler, when he told me the leave of absence was granted, said that my new duties might very well detain me for only a few years, or until the music school was organized and established. Columbia would then, he kindly added, welcome me home again.

Why did I not return to the classroom? After eight years of administrative work I wanted to do so, but it was too late. We were all older. Even my best friends in the Columbia department had grown used to getting on without me, and younger men were rising with their own ideas of the proper way to teach literature. I wanted to go back, but in my heart I knew—I had always known—that it's a mistake to resume, or try to resume, a finished chapter, and equally a mistake to outstay your time. The fact that I should enjoy giving more lectures until the retiring age of sixty-five was no evidence that the lectures would be better than those I had already given, nor even as good. It seemed wiser to start fresh and give all my time to writing.

4

I packed my bags for the lecture tour in a confused or mystical mood. Though I was acquainted with my itinerary, I expected and hoped that somewhere in the Southwest, after the Mississippi had been crossed, I should come on vestiges of France in the New world. My ignorance of geography and history was deplorable. Some years later I saw New Orleans, but on this tour it was not Old France I learned about but Old Spain and Old Mexico.

5

The tour was exciting from the first, with cordial audiences and a very pleasant sense that my books had prepared the warm greeting for me, but not till I reached Pittsburgh on February 20 were the mystical expectations justified. Some reminders of the past greeted me there. I had known the Director of the Carnegie Institute of Technology from the years before the war when he had been Headmaster of Tome School, Port Deposit. Thomas Stockman Baker was a graduate of Johns Hopkins, where he had taught modern languages and where he had become known among his fellow teachers for his knowledge of music. He had a lovely voice. The year before I made this lecture tour, while the Juilliard Board were considering possible candidates for the presidency of the School, I had nominated Dr. Baker and the Board had authorized me to discuss the presidency with him. But he was too deeply interested in the work he had planned at Carnegie Tech.

Several times he had invited me there to give a course of lectures on literature, and in the audience, to my great pleasure, I invariably saw Bishop Boyle. A visit to Pittsburgh had come to mean for me good talks with the Bishop and Dr. Baker. I now expected my lecture visit to be made memorable chiefly by them, but just before

I started from New York I received an invitation to stay with Professor and Mrs. Edmond Esquerré at 708 St. James Street. Though I had not yet met them I felt that they were old friends since René Galland,[1] who knew them well, had often spoken of them. Professor Esquerré came from Toulouse. He was Professor of Physical Education at the Institute of Technology. I had a correct premonition that the hospitality of the Esquerré home would be unique, but I did not realize how unique.

I arrived the afternoon of the twentieth, carrying my two heavy bags and rather hoping for some placid hours before going on to Altoona that evening. Helen Esquerré greeted me at the door with her dynamic temperament. Inside the house I could hear the hum of much conversation. As I recall, Professor Esquerré seized my bags, and before I could take off my heavy coat I was pushed into the living room filled with people. Aside from vague recollection of a delicious cup of tea, and many attractive ladies all talking at once, I recall nothing of that afternoon. Toward the end of it Professor Esquerré reminded me that to make my engagement at Altoona I ought to start at once. I shaved and dressed for the evening, and dashed off unburdened with luggage. Helen Esquerré called after me that when I got home around midnight I'd find some refreshment in the dining room.

I had never been in Altoona. I knew it was one of the shop centers of the Pennsylvania Railroad, but whether railroad engineers and their families devoted their spare time to literature and the arts, was as yet concealed from me.

When I reached the lecture hall I saw at once that I had an unusual audience, rather large and decidedly interested in me and my books. As soon as I began to speak, I picked out here and there faces that seemed especially alert, and turned my oratory, as a gratified lecturer will do, toward those encouraging spots. In the rear of the hall stood a tall, aristocratic figure, strangely familiar. The

[1] *The Memory*, p. 249.

fact that he was standing pleased me; the lecture committee had sold more tickets than there were seats. Then I began to place that tall figure in a far-away part of my life. He was John Duer, the younger brother of Sarah, Angelica, and Elizabeth.[2]

John, I knew, had become a civil engineer, and was on the staff of the Pennsylvania Railroad. He had married, but until that moment I did not realize that he lived in Altoona. He had come to hear me, remembering how as boys we made a system of signals, and tried to send messages across the gap of the old Boulevard which divided the large Duer estate from the much more humble Erskine property. My sisters and I used to think his father looked something like an English earl—not that we had ever seen an English earl. Now John Duer reminded me of his tall parent. He had the same erect carriage, the same keen expression, the same trick of laughing silently when he was pleased. What else occurred during the evening I do not remember, but after the lecture John presented me to his wife, a girl with good looks and an affectionate heart, I should judge, who greeted me warmly, as having been a part of her husband's boyhood.

On the train back to Pittsburgh I was thinking not of the lecture but of Weehawken and of Grace Church,[3] where Father and Mr. Duer worked together for good causes, while their children watched, admired, and silently applauded.

There was indeed a supper waiting for me in the Esquerré home, and Helen Esquerré, still vivid and tireless, ready for a report of the Altoona lecture, and for talk into the early morning about things more personal.

She was a remarkable character, a brilliant mind, and a highly emotional temperament. In her ancestry there must have been a strain of Irish. Her wit was really wisdom, rather than a display of bright sayings. She liked my early novels, but thought she detected in them here and there an imperfect acquaintance with

[2] *The Memory*, p. 53.
[3] *The Memory*, p. 49.

human nature. Whatever she said about the stories concealed perhaps, but not too completely, the wish to probe into me. Why had
I written those books? Why had they taken such a grip of novel
readers that I was now lecturing in Pittsburgh and Altoona?

I regret to recall that on that evening I was abnormally preoccupied with myself, with the memory of my early life, with more
recent adventures, with all my problems of the moment, both educational and personal. Helen Esquerré, brilliant talker, was even a
more brilliant listener. I knew I was talking too much, but her
listening drew me out.

Bishop Hugh Boyle of Pittsburgh had long been an admiration
of mine, and the Esquerrés belonged to his Cathedral congregation.
My recollection of the topics we handled that night includes theology, the mysteries of feminine character, and the errors of college
professors. The next morning we breakfasted around noon, and
there was more talk, this time with Edmond Esquerré assisting. He
was a distinct personality, rather American through long residence
on this side of the ocean, but unalterably French in some of the
finest French traits. He refused to be disturbed by the postwar
younger generation; rather, he reminded us of old parallels to anything in youth which then distressed elders. Human nature would
always be the same—very fortunately if we studied human nature,
unfortunately if we permitted human nature always to take us by
surprise. He was as thoughtful as René Galland, but his mind had
a keener edge, and it cut deeper.

When I left Pittsburgh on that visit it was with the hope of meeting Edmond Esquerré frequently for the rest of my life, but he died
in June, 1933, and the house on St. James Street, as he and his wife
maintained it, is only a memory.

Yet I continue to feel its influence. Helen Esquerré was so hospitable to Pittsburgh lecturers and to worth-while visitors from
abroad, that wherever I have encountered them after their Pittsburgh stay I was fairly sure they would tell me of the Esquerré
kindnesses.

It was to Helen Esquerré that I owed my first meeting with the
Grand Duchess Marie, when that remarkable woman was first lecturing and writing in this country. She knew my books and expressed some wish to meet me, probably in courteous answer to
Helen Esquerré's suggestion. I had a letter from Pittsburgh informing me that the Grand Duchess would be in New York at a certain
date, and Helen Esquerré would be here at the same time. They
lunched with me at the Berkshire Hotel, and a friendship which I
have long prized began with that meeting.

"I never met a duchess before in my life. How am I supposed to
address her?"

She told me. "Your name is John, is it not? Mine is Marie."

6

The Washington audience was large and very stimulating, but
my engagements on the Atlantic seaboard, however pleasant, taught
me nothing new, with the exception of a breakfast in Lynnhaven.
My schedule turned north again for a day or two to take in Balti-
more, Haddonfield, and Trenton. At Trenton I stayed overnight
with my cousin, Mrs. Charles Gummere, and Bess Scarborough
came on from Philadelphia to increase the number of my local
backers.

At Richmond I had looked forward to meeting the audience after
the lecture, but a slip-up in the schedule-making of the lecture agent
compelled me to find a racing car and be off as soon as I finished
my talk, in order to make an evening lecture at Norfolk. Arriving
rather breathless, I hoped to find a hotel room, but Mary Sinton
Leitch, the poet, and her husband, John David Leitch, drove in from
Lynnhaven for the talk, and carried me off afterward to their fascinating place on the Lynnhaven shore.

In spite of weariness I enjoyed this continued travel by car over
sandy roads in the warm Virginia night. Mrs. Leitch I knew from
Poetry Society meetings in New York. Mr. Leitch I met then for

the first time. A very interesting man who had a pre-Prohibition supply of indescribably delicious rum, a vestige, I suppose, of his early seagoing days. Within sound of the bay we sipped nectar and exchanged yarns till almost dawn. After a short but sound sleep I was up packing my bag before breakfast and studying the timetable for my train to Lynchburg and Greensboro.

Breakfast consisted of coffee and Lynnhaven oysters right out of the water. Normally I should have considered this diet precarious after a hard day and a night with little sleep. But to my surprise and delight the oysters were just what I wanted, and when Mr. Leitch drove me to my train, I was rested and ready for more adventure.

7

I think of the Norfolk visit as closing the Atlantic seaboard part of my tour. From Lynchburg on I turned toward the Gulf of Mexico and gradually toward the West. The places where I spoke in the cotton-raising States of the Deep South made real for me some chapters of our history. In one place, for example, I was invited to visit the owner of an old plantation who served tea for her guests in a small, charmingly redecorated building which before the Civil War had been the slave infirmary.

My hostess, a direct descendant of the original owners, was a loyal advocate of the Old South and all its ways. In particular she fastened on me, as coming from New York. We Northerners, she told me in words of one syllable, knew nothing about the South nor about the Southern temperament. In our treatment of the Negro race, she explained, we were preparing trouble for the very people we thought we were helping. Anyone born in the Old South—that is, any true Southern lady or gentleman—knew by instinct the kind of help the Negro race desired. Slavery had been a benign institution. In her own family, for example, so far back as memory could reach, the slaves had been devoted to their owners, invariably contented and loyal. When Mr. Lincoln made his tragic mistake and set them free, the Negroes on that particular plantation may not have gone into mourning, but they certainly grieved. She had often heard her people describe their pitiful dejection.

The lady's eloquence made unnecessary any comment—perhaps I may say, made comment difficult, even impossible. While she laid down the true doctrine of beatitude in servitude, I enjoyed her excellent tea, and refrained from asking her why she had left the original iron bars in the windows of the slave hospital.

. I wanted to see more of the old plantations, but even in winter the humidity in that region was extremely trying. I began to feel happy again when my schedule brought me to Texas. Louis Alber had scheduled for me a number of excursions into Oklahoma, but for the most part my route westward lay through Texas.

In Oklahoma City I had my first sight of American Indians in large numbers. They were not at all as I had imagined. Most of them, it seemed, had struck oil, and were now riding in their automobiles. Their features were still noble, but I was sorry to observe that the general use of the car was spoiling their figures; most of the men were fat. It was raining when I entered Oklahoma, and I made a note that the first American Indian I ever saw was wearing rubbers.

Before my lecture a gentleman called on me to pay his respects, a well-bred, very English person, who explained at once his reason for waiting upon me. He was a Scot and his name was Erskine. He had come to Oklahoma in his youth, had prospered and was happy there. His children too liked the country, and his son had married an Indian princess.

I pricked up my ears. "How do the races get on in matrimony?"

"Oh, well enough! My son and his wife are extremely happy. I'm the one who suffers a little—at family reunions. I can't help feeling that my son's in-laws and the rest of the tribe think the girl married beneath her."

At another place in Oklahoma I lectured on old Greek myths associated with Helen of Troy. At the end of the evening the audience·thanked me as they went out, everyone shaking my hand with Oklahoma cordiality. With my mind on a train to catch, I used the handshake to pull each person along and hurry up the line, but one lady whose face was obscured by a broad hat clung to me long enough to ask a question.

"You pronounce the name of Helen's daughter with the accent on the second syllable, *Her-mí-o-ne*. Could it not be pronounced with the accent on the third, *Her-mi-óne?*"

"Undoubtedly it could." She hurried off into the night.

A few days later I met her again in Texas, this time wearing a small hat. Of course I did not recognize her, but she fastened on me at sight and continued her inquiry into the name of Helen's daughter.

"But why does that interest you, Madame?"

"It's *my* name, and I always thought it was Her-mi-óne. It's something of a shock to know I had it wrong all these years."

"But how did you get that name out here on the prairie?"

"I was Mother's last attempt to have a son. I have twelve sisters. When *I* came along it was embarrassing. Mother had run out of girls' names. She wrote to the schoolteacher who had boarded with us the winter before, and the schoolteacher wrote on a post card this name, Her-mí-o-ne or Her-mi-óne. Mother didn't know how to pronounce it, and neither did I. But there's a worse side to it; as I grew up I modeled my character upon what I supposed was the character of Hermióne. Now I have your book, and I know it wasn't Hermióne I was imitating, but Helen. I feel rather mixed up."

CHAPTER XVII

Frontiers and Horizons

___

1

I EXPECTED to find in Texas a vigorous and colorful way of life, but nothing—I apologize for my ignorance—markedly intellectual. Perhaps I had taken too seriously the legends of Pecos Bill. Dallas, the first city I saw, disappointed me. It seemed too grown-up and sophisticated, the homes were too civilized, the streets were beautiful in an anemic style. No herds of cattle supplied what I should have accepted as the authentic Texas note; no cowboys hitched their ponies outside convenient bars. I told myself the real thing must be waiting in Forth Worth. My Dallas friends encouraged this idea. Since my notion of essential Texas included a good deal of roughness and toughness, they were willing that I should look for it in the neighboring town.

But Forth Worth proved as receptive to lectures as any place I visited. Beyond question the famous cow center was well supplied with cows, but the inhabitants had evidently improved their minds far beyond meat. The range of their ideas would have done credit to a woman's literary club in Westchester or the suburbs of Boston. Moreover, almost any place in Texas may serve as introduction to the academic or university life of the state. From my lecture engagement at Dallas the Professor of English at Baylor University took me in his car to Waco, over smooth roads but at a speed which recalled the ride from Richmond to Norfolk.

Professor A. Joseph Armstrong is immortalized at Baylor by the Browning collection which he brought together and gave to the University. On the Texas prairie he taught the poetry of Robert Browning with such enthusiasm that for his former pupils, now grown men and women, the volumes in the handsome bookcases are charged with memories of English poetry and its Texas interpreter.

I lectured at Baylor University and first saw the Browning collection on March 14, 1928. This afternoon, August 25, 1947, I have been reading the account of the Browning Room in the *Baylor University Bulletin,* Vol. L, No. 3. Dr. Armstrong continues to assemble whatever concerns the poet and his fame, first editions, translations, letters, portraits. There will soon be a special building at Waco to house these treasures, gathered and donated by many students and other admirers of the devoted teacher who has lived to see his own zeal for Browning take root and spread in the Texas landscape and the Texas character.

I liked the attitude of Professor Armstrong's students, all the more because I soon had reason to believe it is an attitude common to Texas youth. It may be doubted whether any of them endanger their health by overstudy, but they are alert, they can use their minds, they get all the fun possible out of their reading and their classes, and whether because they are protected by their natural irreverence, or for some better reason, they seem to stand in no awe of their teachers. Perhaps they do respect those who are scholarly and know how to impart knowledge, but in general they assign professors to their proper place among the other facts of life, along with aunts and uncles, parents, deans and college presidents, treating them all with courtesy, with wise tolerance, and when they deserve it, with affection.

I found this attractive attitude among the young people who came to hear me at Austin, and later at Lubbock. The older folk who arranged the lecture at the State University and at the new institution further west were curious to hear me, but somewhat on guard against my books. The students, however, made me feel that I belonged to their generation, and had written the books for them.

At Austin the fine buildings and the many evidences of an affluence rarely associated with colleges or universities, ought to have made a unique impression, but I was becoming accustomed to Texas. The University had a faculty far above the average, and the Library contained some extraordinary collections. I spent an afternoon in the Wrenn Library of rare Elizabethan and seventeenth century items—priceless books which might be looked for in the British Museum or the Bodleian. With this and other material to work on, with excellent scholars teaching English literature, the University, I thought might soon be attracting some of the special students who used to visit England in the course of their Ph.D. thesis-writing.

In short, the University of Texas promised no end of good things for American education. The State had youth, imagination, courage and wealth. Wealth, beyond question. The other qualities I was to learn more about, though not on this particular tour.

In the years 1931-1935, Bucknell University at Lewisburg, Pennsylvania, had a young president who made other colleges more than a little envious. He had a way of making education practical, in the best sense. Whatever the subject, he wanted it studied for use. He knew the dry rot to which all schools are liable, and at Bucknell, so rumor said, he was inspiring students and teachers alike by constant demonstrations that knowledge is power if—and only if—we put it to practice. He invited me to lecture at Bucknell, September 22, 1933. At the morning convocation one of the students played the piano, very well indeed. I learned that the young President insisted that all who had talents should exercise them. Singers, violin and piano players, took their turn in morning chapel. At first the students resisted, but one morning the President announced an operatic selection and said he would sing it himself. The boys and girls did not know he had trained to make music his profession. His performance that morning rather swept them off their feet, and those who could sing or play a little, began to think well of themselves.

His name was Homer Price Rainey, and at his inauguration in December 1939 as President of Texas University, I spoke, at his request, on the place of the Fine Arts in a State University. I hope I said nothing to blight his career. When his liberal ideas incurred the animosity of his Board of Regents, a few years later, the professors took his part, and so did the students. To have the cordial support of brains and youth, ought to spell success for any president, but the Regents dismissed him, and so far as education is concerned the richly endowed institution has remained in a festering condition ever since. Dr. Rainey is now President of Stephens College, Columbia, Missouri.

When I visited Austin on my lecture tour I had no knowledge of Denton, the near-by town where the North Texas State Teachers College is located, and the Texas State College for Women. But in the next few years I came to know quite well the College for Women and its remarkable president, John Herman Hubbard. On the afternoon of Dr. Rainey's inauguration, President Hubbard was naturally one of the important educators present and I rode with him afterward to Denton for a few days of lecturing at what I believe is one of the finest colleges in our country.

Dr. Hubbard has essentially the same ideas as Dr. Rainey; he wishes his students to get a complete training for their life, for the world in which they are to live, for the world which their talent and temperament ought to create. The curriculum includes the usual academic subjects, but also it provides instruction in the fine and useful arts, and it gives what is usually called vocational training. The unusual ability of President Hubbard discloses itself in the complete integration of all these opportunities for learning. The girls with musical ability, for example, play and sing in the college orchestra or the college choir, and their training is excellent, but neither they nor their teachers expect them necessarily to enter the musical profession. The College does expect them to carry back into Texas homes the ability to lead happy and accomplished lives, and to elevate the tone of the general culture.

The college fees are moderate, but the total for tuition, board and a room in the dormitories is often more than a student can afford. In such cases the students register on a cooperative basis, doing their own housekeeping. The necessity is turned into a rare opportunity. If the girl must make her bed and tidy up her room, the college trains her to do this work in the easiest and most efficient way. If she is earning her education by assisting in the kitchen or in the large dining room, again she is trained in the art of cooking and serving food. Other vocational schools might charge a tuition fee for this education but the Texas College for Women remembers that the student is contributing to the general work of the institution. The cost of tuition and board for the cooperative students at Denton is fantastically low, and what they learn is valuable indeed.

One original idea of President Hubbard's I must pause to describe. The daily chapel exercises are held in an immense auditorium which accommodates about five thousand. Dr. Hubbard felt that something was missing from so large a meeting place. He engaged an architect to design a small Gothic structure in the woods at one end of the campus. Only the shell of a diminutive chapel was put up. He then invited the students to finish the building as they would like it to be. Those who were studying mural decoration agreed on a plan for the walls, others designed and executed stained glass for the windows, those who studied woodcarving designed and made the pews, others designed and made the electric lighting fixtures. When I first saw the chapel, a squad of students were laying a mosaic in the floor. The chapel contained a small organ and the other fixtures which belong to such an edifice, but Dr. Hubbard told me he wished to hold no services in the place, rather he hoped that the students from one academic generation to another, would stroll through the beautiful woods to their chapel, and enter for a few minutes of meditation, self-examination and planning. Here he would like them to cultivate their dreams.

The chapel need never be finished. Successive groups of students may in time bring it to perfection, but he will be satisfied, he said, if the girls who made the first glass for the stained windows, some day bring their daughters to see what Mother was thinking of when she was at school. From the little chapel might spring an incalculable tradition of beauty and noble aspirations.

Because my first tour through Texas led to later visits and fruitful friendships, I have advanced the chronology of my story in order to speak of Dr. Rainey and Dr. Hubbard. I wish I had room here to describe repeated visits to Dallas and Fort Worth, to places in western Texas, and in recent years to El Paso. But I must say a word now about San Antonio, not merely for its own charming sake, but because it first taught me the close alliance of our history with that of Mexico, and the richness of the contribution which Old Spain made and still makes to our heritage.

When I was leaving Austin after my lecture at the University, the friends who drove me to the railroad station asked where I had reserved a room. I've forgotten the name of the hotel, but not the look of disapproval when they heard it.

"You're not staying at the Menger?"

I knew nothing of the Menger.

"Then you simply are not an educated man. If you don't go to the Menger, we'll never speak to you again."

So I went to the Menger, and have been grateful to my friends ever since. As most Americans know, who know anything about Texas—the Menger Hotel stands on the Plaza a few hundred feet from the historic Alamo. During the Second World War the old building suffered from neglect, but when I was last there, a few months ago, it was beautifully restored to its old magnificence, and in spite of alterations, to something of its old spaciousness. In the rooms, especially the dining room, the service is supplied by men and women whose parents have been part of the Menger household for several generations.

Perhaps the Alamo, which naturally is a shrine for Americans, especially for Texans, is gradually becoming a shrine also for Mexicans. If this impression is correct, it is something to be thankful for. The heroic dead who fell in the little fortress-church were far outnumbered by the besiegers whom their bullets stopped. Fighting on both sides was desperate, and the motives, we all can now see, were patriotic. When I first saw the Alamo, and every time I have seen it again, I have brought away the conviction that it is a monument not to the past but to the bright future of Mexico and the United States.

2

My week in California began on March 26 with an afternoon lecture in Pasadena, followed by an evening lecture at Los Angeles. The next morning I spoke again in Los Angeles. The morning of the twenty-eighth I spoke in Hollywood, and in the evening at Santa Ana. The evening of the twenty-ninth I spoke in San Diego, and the morning of the thirtieth I gave my final lecture in Los Angeles.

This was my first acquaintance with the Western Coast, and I immediately fell in love with the Pacific Ocean, which I insist is entirely different from the Atlantic, even to those who merely look at it from the shore. If San Antonio with its history made me think of the American future, California sent my imagination working toward the Far East. There is much Spanish influence of course in Lower California, but even in 1928 when we were not thinking of the Second World War, the Pacific Coast suggested dreams and broodings, not about where we came from, but where we were going.

My week of lectures would have been difficult except for the kindness of my classmate William C. de Mille, who invited me to stay with him and to use his car and driver for transportation. At the moment he was living alone in a picturesque house in Hollywood on Monteel Road. This was just before his marriage to Clara Beranger. Since Clara was for the moment in the East, William permitted me to console him. I hope I did. After having driven in his car to my lecture, whether at Los Angeles or at Santa Ana, I would reach Monteel Road at midnight or later, and William in his comfortable dressing gown would be waiting on his attractive stone porch, where we could sit and enjoy the lights of the vast city, or the further lights twinkling from Catalina Island.

I have happy memories of that visit in the Monteel Road house and still happier memories of later visits to William and Clara in their present home near the ocean on Gillis Street. Whether it came from the first impact of California, or from the pleasure I had in William's hospitality, I cherish a peculiar affection for the town of Hollywood and the city of Los Angeles, which not all of my Eastern friends can understand. The feeling is not associated in any way with the motion picture industry, though I admire those who developed the most influential medium of expression which mankind enjoys, criticizes or envies. But at that time the Pacific Coast was more fascinating to me than any motion picture. What has happened since, does not change my opinion.

The atmosphere of the Monteel house was influenced in no small degree by Amando, William's Filipino cook, who prepared the most superb dinners. William asked some friends to come in the only evening which was possible for all of us. The fact that I had a lecture that night in Los Angeles, did not disturb Amando nor any of the guests. There were Wilfred and Vera Buckland, and Cornelia Runyan. Cornelia now lives thirty miles down the Coast, literally at the ocean's edge. Wilfred and Vera died only a short time ago. As I write, they all seem alive. I left the dinner table that evening when the feast had barely started, and returned two hours later to enjoy the food Amando had kept warm for me, and to play the piano for another hour or so. After that we just talked, and what talk!

California audiences all made the same impression on me. They were not intellectual. They certainly were keen, interested, and intelligent, but their ruling passions were quite obviously not connected with books. They made me feel that if my lecture made any allusion to literature, I was breaking new ground for them.

It has been my good fortune to spend much time during the succeeding years in Hollywood, where I enjoy the society of the picture people, but am increasingly amazed at the success with which they resist all inducements to read a book. This is particularly true of the studio heads, who after paying generous sums for the right to put a novel on the screen, rely on a specialist in their studio to read the story and tell them what it's about. They themselves claim that their work kills the desire to read, but since other Californians don't read either, I conclude that the climate, though extremely favorable to the invention of kindly but half-baked philosophies, is discouraging to authorship.

I noticed on my first visit and have studied the phenomenon more thoroughly since then, that the philosophers of Los Angeles and Hollywood prefer oral to written communication. They listen courteously to your private philosophy, by way of earning the right to tell you theirs. This done, they hurry off to spread the true gospel over the next willing listener. I once met on a hotel porch an apparently sane person who asked me what I thought of the Pacific Coast. I said I thought it was remarkably favorable to new philosophies. Her smile led me to believe for a moment that we understood each other. "New philosophies," I expanded, "which have been kicking around this battered world for thousands of years, until whatever common sense may once have been in them, has worn pretty thin."

"Isn't it so!" she agreed. "Most of the things you listen to here are silly. But not all. Now, my own belief, for example——" She was off on an exposition of her private philosophy, which was worse than any of the others I had heard.

My own philosophy is that California sunlight is too stimulating for any but strong heads.

3

After I left Los Angeles I stopped next at Santa Barbara, then a popular winter resort with the English. My lecture was given in a private house before what seemed to be a literary club. The audience were all British, cultured, and well traveled. If they hadn't traveled six thousand miles that winter to enjoy the California sun, they would have spent the season on the Riviera. The pleasant evening they gave me seems now a memory from a past age. The leisured class in every country has thinned out. Great Britain now contributes no considerable patronage to the Riviera or to Santa Barbara.

An extremely crowded day at San Francisco recalled me to the prophetic aspects of western America. The romantic city on its steep hills, still wore much of the picturesqueness described by its admirers from pioneer days onward. But what attracted me most was the wonderful Bay with ships pouring through the Golden Gate, and the traffic between the Orient and the West sounding a dull roar along the water front.

After a morning visiting book stores and giving interviews to reporters, I was entertained at lunch in a tall narrow house set on the side of a steep hill. The room in which we ate was long and narrow, and from the windows we looked down on the Bay and watched the ships go and come. At the table were Alfred Hertz, the symphonic conductor, Gertrude Atherton, the novelist, and several painters. I wish I could remember now the wise things they said, but what stays with me is the impression that San Francisco had little to do with Los Angeles, and perhaps only a casual relation to the United States. The town had been built up by the gold seekers, and the artists and novelists who joined the miners were seeking only another kind of gold. The city was and is, I suspect, located at the end of the rainbow. The inhabitants still hope that the rainbow extends much further than dull folk suppose.

With San Francisco not yet fully explored or digested, I hurried on to the quite different kinds of energy in Portland and Seattle. In the latter place Bruce Elmore was waiting for me with his own special kind of warm welcome. Bruce had been my classmate at Columbia along with William de Mille. After he finished his four years at the College of Physicians and Surgeons, he practiced surgery for a while in the Navy, and then moved as far west as possible to get a start in the new world. Because our lives had wandered far apart, this was the first time I laid eyes on him since we said goodbye at Commencement. He had a charming home at 1114 Boylston Avenue; and his wife Annette, his daughter Mary, and his son Bruce, all made the home cheery. Why not? They were all red-headed. There also was a younger boy, Dan.

Bruce was on the staff of the Roosevelt Clinic of Seattle at the top of his profession but he had seen some rough going. When he first arrived in Seattle, he told me, the inhabitants were ridiculously independent of surgeons. They occasionally did break an arm or a leg, but they would set the broken bones themselves with the aid of a bent wire, and if the mended limb was crooked, the neighbors recognized a familiar experience.

After some months, Bruce was ready to take down his shingle and go home to the effete East. Then one morning a heavy truck ran over a little girl before his very door. The poor child was so badly smashed up that the truck driver, the policeman and the sympathetic onlookers did not waste time ringing the doctor's doorbell, but sent for the coroner.

Bruce, hurrying down his front steps, saw that the child was not yet dead and might not have to die. He carried her into his office, gave her first aid and nursed her back beyond immediate danger. But after all he was a surgeon, and watching her lying there with her hands shattered and her face disfigured, he began to plan a miracle. She was the daughter of an Italian who perhaps could not afford lengthy operations, but Bruce asked for the privilege of working his miracle for nothing, and the father consented. One by one the ten fingers were straightened out and made to work again as Nature intended. But the girl had been very pretty; what good would it do her now to have ten capable fingers, if her face remained disfigured? For almost two years Bruce lifted a piece of skin here and put it down again there, moving everything that was movable to the spot where it would do the most good.

At the end of the long ordeal the young patient walked out of Bruce Elmore's house as active and as good-looking as she ever had been. Her grateful father knelt on the sidewalk to kiss Bruce's hand, and was sent away with a violent admonition to forget it, and not make a fool of himself. After that, Bruce was established in Seattle.

4

Perhaps it is ungracious, after the hospitality I received on the rest of the tour, but truth compels me to say that the journey westward through Texas and up along the Pacific Coast made the lectures in the West and Middlewest an anticlimax. I have lectured frequently in the Middlewest since then and on every visit I have learned to appreciate some of the great qualities to which I had been blinded by the places on the Pacific Coast. I cannot now remember the lecture I gave on my tour at the University of Minnesota, for example, but I have spoken there frequently and have twice played concertos with the Minneapolis Orchestra in the great hall of the University, and I was glad to hear in Minneapolis the name of Madame Schöen-René mentioned with affectionate gratitude. For many years she had taught singing in the Minnesota landscape, before the formation of the Juilliard faculty brought her to New York.

All my miscellaneous memories of this long journey are bound together by a few recurring experiences. In most schools and universities the officer who introduced me to the audience was a colleague, an old friend. My old friends, as I soon discovered, did not understand *The Private Life of Helen of Troy,* and perhaps did not understand me, since they had trouble explaining how I came to write it. At Vanderbilt University, Nashville, Tennessee, my dear friend Professor Edwin Mims presided, and on the platform with him was Professor Curtis Walker, one of the inmates of the *Maison Marsh* in my Amherst days. The introductory speech was an ingenious attempt to prepare the listeners to hear something solid or something foolish, whichever way I might break out.

At the University of Cincinnati, the demand for the lecture was so great that I gave it twice, in the afternoon and the evening, both times introduced by Professor Frank Chandler, old friend from Columbia days. I still have the manuscript of his extremely funny introduction, full of warm friendship but certainly not of confidence in what I might say. In Cincinnati as in Nashville, the bewilderment of old friends was a challenge which I gladly accepted. I don't think my lecture was solemn, but I know it was crammed with more solid information about Helen of Troy and other legendary characters than those particular colleagues had ever dreamed of. Well, I started with the conviction that professors need educating and my own knowledge of American life and American character was enriched by this tour.

CHAPTER XVIII

Education for my Children

1

M Y GREATEST success as teacher and educator I had with my own children. There were special and extremely favorable conditions, to stand between me and conceit. If I recount the process now, it is chiefly to regret that I did less well with other students. I hope also that the incidents may throw light on principles which, like other teachers, I have always believed in and groped for.

When I speak of the favorable conditions of their training, I mean the advantages they had, as children of a college teacher, to hear the talk of educated people, and to learn from earliest youth what subjects the scholarly discuss among themselves, either because they like to, or because they think they should.

My children were encouraged to listen to whatever our friends cared to say. I doubt if professors are less sincere than other folk, more given to posing. Yet it is natural that among those who have explored and profess to lead the intellectual life, there should be some who put on airs; they would relax into a natural stupidity or vulgarity if they thought it professionally safe. I wanted my children to recognize the authentic fineness in the utterance of trained minds and also the telltale insincerities, if any appeared.

Should a school undertake to teach a subject, or to teach the child? I tried to educate my children in many ways, to some of which I could give no ready name. I hoped to develop and strengthen character, to train their minds, to teach them to think. The upshot of education, I believed, should be a greater articulateness, an approach to complete expression. If I said I wanted my children to be artists, the statement would be true, but also it might mislead. They learned to play the piano and to sing, to dance, to swim, to play tennis, to ride a horse. These are not necessarily arts but they may be. For every temperament there is one language in which expression may become complete and satisfying. In some cases the one language is found only by experiment. Young people should be encouraged to try everything. Familiarity with a medium is a permanent advantage, even though the destined language lies elsewhere. My children did not become pianists, or singers, or professional dancers, or remarkable swimmers, or tennis stars, or horse-show performers.

But in these exercises which they enjoy as amateurs, they learned the two qualities of character which are essential in the practice of any art—they learned courage, without which no one ever speaks out; and determination to go through to the end. I once told my son, when he was a child, that I was distressed to observe his efforts to put his toy hammer through the windowpane. But I was even more distressed that he abandoned the project because the glass was stronger than he thought. I showed him the right angle at which to strike the glass in order to smash it, thereby recovering, I hope, some firmness of character. I added, however, that if he did succeed in breaking the glass, my own character would probably weaken; I would applaud his firmness of purpose, but he might be sent to bed without any supper.

If a student in school or college does not know what he or she wants to do, the teacher can do little for him. I doubt if lack of decision at any age beyond ten is curable. When the child goes to school his parents go with him in spirit, and unless they always knew what they wanted, their offspring is likely to repeat their wobbling to the end of his days. But at least he need not be an inarticulate wobbler. We may hope to make of him so much of a personality that he can express his temporary likes and dislikes, and describe intelligently his confusion.

The necessity to be articulate is ignored in American education. Many of our children possess as it were from the cradle the gift of nailing an idea in a swift and just phrase. But the family rebuke the young artist by the questionable formula that children should be seen and not heard. In general my experience would suggest that children have talents of expression more often than good looks. Far be it from me to say that their parents are not handsome. I would merely recall to elders as well as to youth, the ancient wisdom of the Greeks, that the end of living, as of education, is first to fill the head and the heart, and then to acquire the skill to express what is in them. In the Homeric world, the strong silent man was not easily distinguishable from the uneducated or the foolish. Achilles was trained to be a speaker of words, as well as a doer of deeds.

Just when my elder child, Graham, discovered that he was an artist, I cannot say exactly. From his sixth or seventh year when his sister was only an infant, he must have begun to make sketches prompted by an impulse which is beyond explaining. I went to France in the First World War when Anna had hardly learned to walk. When I returned at the end of almost two years, Graham had learned to draw. Several of his letters to me at the front contained pictures of things or events which he found easier to describe that way than in words.

In the late summer of 1919 after my return, I spent long hours telling him about the landscape of France, the straight tree-shaded roads, the vine-covered cottages. Since he wanted a picture in every story I illustrated with water-color sketches. From that time he painted constantly in water colors, to the delight of friends and relatives, since his skill as a painter soon exceeded mine. But some instinct led him to use crayons more and more frequently. It became his habit to carry at all times a heavy black crayon and a pad of paper. Whenever he was listening to anyone he sketched as he listened. When his sister was convalescing from an illness at the age of three—he was then eight—I sat by her bed reading a story to her. He stood in the doorway attracted by the story, but also perhaps by the opportunity to sketch. He thought so little of the drawing he made that he dropped it on the floor when he left for some other room. I picked it up, and it rests safely in my scrapbook. In a few strong lines he indicated his sister's head resting on the pillow, slightly turned to listen, and my back and head bent over the book.

When he was between eleven and twelve I talked to him about the Art Students League, describing the work and fun that artists have always found in a studio, giving him discreet reports of the charms of the Left Bank of Paris and of the virtues which under the best circumstances artists have practiced and admired in Bohemia.

When his curiosity and his enthusiasm were thoroughly ignited, I entered him in the Art Students League, where he soon qualified for the life classes. He continued to spend his mornings at this work until he transferred his studies to Paris.

My reasons for getting him into the life classes so early were two: In the first place I wanted him to feel that those who study art are mature and serious. I expected his fellow students to be always much older than he. The experience of studying side by side with mature boys and girls ripened his mind fast, as I hoped it would. My other reason for putting him in the life class was the desire to have him approach the surmises of adolescence and meet the first impact of sex through the avenue of beauty—through the artist's proper concern with the human body. I didn't like to have my boy repeat my experience, and learn wonderful facts of life through the dirty hints and sniggering of the dirty-minded among his schoolmates.

Graham must have been fortunate in the students he consorted with at the League. Most of them were studying painting and drawing with the intention of making art their profession. It was good for him to learn early that art for an artist is a serious business, calling for devoted and conscientious work. In his first discovery that it was a serious business, and in his equally important discovery that the human body should be studied reverently but thoroughly, he provided the family with some unexpected excitements. One afternoon when Mrs. Nicholas Murray Butler, the President's wife, was calling, he came into the room and paid his respects in the best small-boy style, and then retired to a corner and followed the conversation with apparent interest, but he had his sketch paper in his hand, and from moment to moment he would hold up his pencil as though to check the measurements of the visitor. He might have been drawing her portrait, but he wasn't. After she left, he remarked sympathetically, "As far as I can see, that woman's pelvis is about three inches larger than normal."

2

Graham prepared for college at the Horace Mann School, where he indulged a normal boy's taste for sports; his specialty was long-distance running, and he stretched his legs over most of that part of Riverdale. I was glad to encourage this strenuous exercise so long as no one asked me to run. If sports had turned out to be his ruling passion, I should have felt it my duty not to interfere with Fate, but the interest in art continued no matter how many hours the boy spent on the cinder track. I was greatly relieved when his classmates discovered that he could draw lifelike pictures of the teachers. Month after month the school paper published one of his portraits until the entire faculty had been immortalized.

The educational value of these portraits lay, it seemed to me, in what the boy learned about the problem of printing line drawings on paper of variable softness. He told me night after night at the supper table, and I was careful to listen as though I had never heard these particular facts before, that you can't hope to print a fine line on soft paper; in fact, it is rather wise to draw your picture with the end of the pen-holder, or with a fine brush. It seemed to me to learn the influence which materials have on art is itself a valuable kind of education, and Graham was acquiring it without attendance on any class, and without the assignment of lessons by a teacher.

In 1925, the autumn in which I published *The Private Life of Helen of Troy,* I took my family abroad for a four months' journey through France and Italy. We landed at Bordeaux, traveled slowly along the Mediterranean shore into the northern part of Italy, spent a month in Venice, some weeks in Rome and in Florence, then settled down in Paris for the rest of our vacation. The colors of the Mediterranean shore drove Graham at once to his water colors. He made numerous studies of Mediterranean vistas and of the red-roofed white houses clinging to the cliffs along the coast. Anna, five years younger, demanded a box of water colors in order to make her own pictures, and Graham soon had to look to his laurels. He had a natural sense of color and of design, but Anna had an eye for dramatic settings and bold contrasts. At the end of the whole trip she painted two memory pictures, one of a Venetian bridge, the other of Nôtre Dame in Paris. Every detail of these pictures is incorrect, yet the total impression is surprisingly true. I am not saying that from these childish experiments she learned to draw, but she opened her brother's eyes to certain values she always got, and he, until she nudged him, always missed. They were educating each other, as students should always do.

Before we reached Italy we stopped for a week in Arles, and Graham surprised me by asking if I would get permission for him to make sketches of antique Roman monuments in the local museum—bas reliefs on tombs, fragments of arches and pediments. I had not guessed that he cared for such materials. After some delay we made the acquaintance of the Curator and persuaded him that a child really wished to make studies of Roman architecture and sculpture, and that his wish deserved encouragement. The Curator was a gentle soul, but very conventional. He was hard to convince, only because he had never before seen an American boy who wanted to visit the museum any longer than his parents insisted. But Graham spent hours there daily, and perhaps it was in Arles that his interest in art developed into a passion for architecture.

When we reached Paris he told me firmly that he wished to see no more historic buildings, no more castles, no more famous churches. He wished to spend his time in a good art school, and having heard of the Julien Academy, with its memories of Du Maurier's Three Musketeers of the Brush, he wished to study there and nowhere else. I might have protested that Julien's was not then considered a stronghold of the most advanced methods, but since he wished to go there, attracted by the tradition and by the atmosphere, I arranged for him to enter the school, and for the rest of his Paris stay he worked hard. He had hoped to study painting, but after two or three days he changed to the classes in drawing, and the reason he gave indicated that Julien's had already taught him a good deal. The men around him were far more mature, far more serious in purpose, than his friends at the Art Students League in New York.

"I can draw the model well enough," he said, "if he stands still, but these fellows can draw marvelously even though the model moves, and they can draw the motion."

The advance he made in these few weeks surprised me. Not only his technique grew, but he heard, and gradually understood, the art talk of the Europeans working by his side, who exchanged ideas from Vienna, or Munich, or from the academies in Rome.

As our too-brief holiday drew to an end, we packed our bags to go home for the opening of the spring term. Graham would resume his studies at the Horace Mann School, and in two years he would be a candidate for admission to Columbia College. In the freshman class there would be few with whom he could discuss art. His classmates would not be likely to compare the merits of Brahms and Debussy, nor would he find many with whom to discuss the teaching methods of André L'Hote as over against those still adhered to by the Julien devotees.

When we were settled in our cabin for the return voyage, I told Graham that if he passed his entrance examinations with good marks, he could have his freshman year not at Columbia, but at the Sorbonne. He could attend university classes in the morning, and Julien's in the afternoon. He could spend his evenings reading and studying, and discussing life with the member of the Sorbonne faculty whom I hoped would serve as his tutor or friendly adviser.

Graham carried out his part of the bargain, and thanks to Helen of Troy, I was able to keep my promise. Here is one illustration of the special good fortune which attended my son's education. Not every parent has the luck to write a successful book just before his boy goes to college. Graham's first trip abroad was made on his professor-father's hard-earned savings, but his later visits to Europe were made comfortably possible by my writing. On the other hand, I was fortunate beyond the lot of many parents because my boy knew what he wished to make of his life, and wasted no opportunity I could give him.

In his winter at the Sorbonne and the Julien he progressed remarkably in his art, but even more, it seemed to me, in his knowledge of history, of international relations and of special subjects, such as the domestic law of France. This was the subject matter of one of his courses. He had already learned on his first trip to Paris to speak French with some fluency, and after a brief conversation the French scholar who discoursed on domestic law, accepted him as a student. His other courses were in history and in French literature. The reading which was his homework taught him to concentrate like a European. He learned to remember, and to keep his acquired knowledge in a condition to use. At the end of the year he had thoroughly mastered the language, and he had the point of view not of an American freshman or sophomore, but of a graduate student.

In the early summer after his return home he enrolled in the

Columbia Summer Session. "Since I've never attended an American college," he told me, "and since I want to start in with the sophomore class, I might as well learn as soon as possible what an American university is like."

Following the procedure he had learned at the Sorbonne, he looked over the courses offered in the Columbia catalog and chose one on Montaigne's essays. His curiosity about Montaigne had been roused in Paris, and he wanted to study him thoroughly. The professor in charge of the course, a Frenchman, was delighted.

"Of course you may study with me! In what year of graduate work are you?"

When Graham explained that he wasn't yet an undergraduate, the Frenchman was shocked and disappointed. "But this is a graduate course. I can't admit you."

They had been talking in English, the language the Professor expected all his students to use. But now that he was in danger of colliding with the regulations, Graham switched over into voluble French, and asked in what he was unprepared to profit by the course. When the Professor asked where he had acquired his French, and learned of the visits to France and the recent year at the Sorbonne, he surrendered happily. Graham passed the course with a high grade, to the indignation of the head of the French department, an American—who felt correctly that the regulations of the French courses had been made to seem absurd.

I am afraid I was not just the right person for my son to discuss this problem with. I had rebelled too long against the senseless regimentation of American colleges and universities, to defend now a rule which would admit to the graduate course a student who had taken previous French courses without acquiring an acquaintance with the literature and without learning to speak the language. Yet when a boy appeared who could speak French, and who was widely read, the impulse was to keep him out just because he had not suffered under incompetent language instruction.

I don't know whether or not I was sorry that Graham, coming

back to his own country and to my university after a wholesome winter of contact with European education, had more than one illustration of the difference. He expected to enroll in the School of Architecture after he finished his college course. The Columbia curriculum provided for pre-architects several years of training in drawing. Graham, to inform the Director of Admission of his past record, took him an armful of paintings and drawings, the fruit of his afternoons at Julien's. The proper person in the Admissions office cast a critical eye over his rather large exhibit, and warmed with approval.

"We'll give you credit for all your pre-architecture courses."

"What drawing courses shall I take this coming year?"

"None at all! I just told you—you have credit for all that work."

"But I want to draw! Take back the credit! I have plenty to learn and I'd like to keep at it."

For that the University had no answer. If Graham had not enrolled in the Academy of Design, an institution quite separate from Columbia, he could have done no art study that year. His own verdict has not, I believe, changed with the years; he thinks the ideals of his Alma Mater are less mature than those of some of its students. When he finished his college course and entered the School of Architecture, he was invited, even while a student, to assist in the teaching of drawing. I doubt if at the moment any of his teachers could draw so well. Perhaps they had not been busy from their sixth year, with pad and crayon. Art was their profession, but it wasn't necessarily their language.

3

When Graham finished his course at the architectural school, he carried off a pleasant share of honors, among them a traveling scholarship which would give him a winter of architectural study at the University of Rome. I feared I should never see much of him again, but I had started him on what I had hoped would be a cosmopolitan or international career, and I did not regret the logical unfolding of it. He spent the summer at the University of Perugia to perfect himself in the language, moving to Rome at the beginning of the autumn term. While in Perugia he boarded with a family for whom he cherishes a lasting regard, people of fine and ancient culture, reduced to hardship by the prewar catastrophes of exploited Italy. At the end of Graham's year in Rome he returned for a day or so to Perugia, to visit this family, and to consult the head of it about the best binding for a volume of photographs he was bringing to me, to show the archaeological studies he had made of some ancient bits of masonry. The book is delightfully bound, and when I read the inscription I feel a gush of pride that my son, who can design tall buildings, can also put words together. He may be said to have written here his own diploma as an educated man. With shameless pride I add that perhaps he has here given me my diploma as a good teacher.

"*La preparazione di questo libro e stata fatta col grazioso aiuto del Signor Pieroni. Cosi il libro e non soltanto un esempio del mio lavoro alla Scuola d'Architettura ma anche un ricordo di Perugia e della famiglia nella via della Madonna.*"

Graham had written to me that the University of Rome for the first time would grant a Ph.D. in Architecture, and since this was a gesture by way of compliment to our American academic customs, he thought he should try for the honor. But he had no hope of winning it, since his thesis would be the complete design of a building to go up in Rome, and the specifications must be furnished in the material and labor costs then prevailing in Italy. I wrote back at once to forget the competition and come home. I'd be glad to see him even without an architectural Ph.D. He knew what I thought of Ph.D.'s anyway. Before my letter got to him, a despatch to the *New York Herald Tribune* told me that my boy had won the first Ph.D. in Architecture bestowed by the University of Rome.

He was home again, it seemed, for only a short time before the Second World War broke, and he went back to Italy as an engineer with Aviation. I suppose it was natural that American boys who had studied in Italy should be called to serve in that country, since they spoke the language, and many of those who had studied there were architects. In any event Graham and his buddies kept their thoughts out of the Italian mud by exchanging ideas about the future of American architecture. Before Graham left for the Italian front he had already half decided not to practice his profession further in New York. He hoped to establish himself in a newer and more adventurous world. New York, he said, whether wisely or not I don't know, was rapidly becoming a western frontier of Europe, and in time would attach itself to the worn-out ideas of the Old World. He would rather go to South America, which apparently understood the possibilities of modern architecture, and was, as he had heard from me, youthful at heart.

But after he reached Italy and exchanged ideas with other young architects in the Army, he changed his mind, thanks to what one wise youngster remarked one day.

"No doubt there are opportunities in South America. There were and are opportunities in North America and some of the best minds in Europe have been coming over for a hundred years. Perhaps if they hadn't come, Europe would not now be in its present helpless state."

Graham decided to stick to his native land, but to go west, keeping as far as possible beyond Old World influence. He is now practicing architecture in Reno, Nevada. He and his wife love the country and the people and the pioneer spirit which is still strong there—the building spirit, the disposition to make or re-make a world by imaginative thinking and by hard work.

4

When Anna was three or four years old she decided to be an actress. She has departed from that ideal only in so far as she failed to express in her childhood just what it was she wanted to do in life. She has not, to my mind, the actress's temperament, but the theatre, from all angles, is her great interest. Her acting talent is good, but it is not necessary for her to act as it was for Graham to draw. In school the other girls made her president of their dramatics club, not only because she could take a fairly ambitious part, but because she could stage a play and direct the performance. She prepared at the Horace Mann School to enter Barnard College, but she had no intention, as I well realized, to take the college course. We talked it over, one evening, and made a bargain, more or less, like the one I made with Graham.

"Whether or not you have talent, I don't know, and neither do you, and it's too early to tell. You wish to give your entire life to the stage, as most actors do, but it usually seems to their friends something of a pity that they have had the opportunity to learn only their lines. Let's agree to this; if you pass the entrance examinations into Barnard, I'll help you to make some real preparation for an acting career. The entrance examinations may not seem important, but later they will. If you don't take them, you will always have an inferiority complex; you won't be sure you could have passed them."

She passed with credit, and for good measure registered and began the freshman year, but before Christmas she was acting on Broadway, not serious acting of course—only a walk-on part in a play that needed two or three high school girls to stand around and window-dress the plot. I didn't like that development. She wasn't using her mind. She had too much time on her hands. Her friends were other young things who haunted theatrical Broadway and knew the professional catch-phrases or jargon of unemployed actresses.

To Anna's delight, she was permitted to withdraw from Barnard and study the art of acting with Madame Ouspenskaya. Besides the acting lessons, to which she applied herself with satisfying earnestness, she studied make-up and costuming, and singing and dancing, and she disclosed a readiness to accept in the theatre any job that offered. It is not much of an exaggeration to say that after her two years with Ouspenskaya she was never unemployed, winter or summer. I suppose it was to her advantage that she was not consistently employed in acting. She began with a small chorus part in *Naughty Naught,* the burlesque. She played in summer stock. She had one or two small Broadway parts, and she served as assistant stage manager in theatrical or operatic ventures outside of New York. When the approach of the war began to thin out the ranks, she served in the business office of Lindsey and Crouse. There is little about the theatre, either behind the scenes or in front, that she doesn't know. If her marriage to Russel Crouse had not brought a good playwright into the household, I think she would now be writing plays herself. Or perhaps it is my grandson, Timothy Crouse, who stands in the way of her writing.

But not entirely. Strong as her passion for the theatre will always be, and familiar though she is with every aspect of it, she discloses more and more a strong bent toward writing. She has wit and humor and a marked satiric tendency, a small share of which she ascribes to me.

When she was visiting friends in Hollywood a few years ago, someone asked how she explained her interest in the stage since there had been no actors in her family.

"I know," she replied, "I think it's just the ham in Father coming out."

So far as I am concerned her education is no longer my responsibility. She is in the hands of Russel and Timothy. But Timothy will need my advice. He is only a year old, but a week or so ago Russel and Anna asked me quite seriously what school he should attend. I have gone further. I am almost ready to pick out a college for him. I hope he will make his mark in the newest of new worlds, wherever that will be. I suspect it will rise on the borders of the Pacific Ocean. I hope he'll find a great education there, either in the universities of the mainland or further toward the ancient East, wherever our frontier may push.

Russel and Anna smile tenderly when I say that if Guam becomes a state, it will probably set up the most modern of universities, and I'd like Timothy to study there. Their smiles, I suspect, indicate that my mind is failing even more rapidly than they feared. I regret that Timothy's parents are so conservative. If he reaches my age, he will be living in the year 2015. When John Harvard was at Cambridge, England, who could have imagined a university near Boston, or one in New Haven, or one on Manhattan Island—or one near San Francisco Bay? I remain faithful to my own temperament. Timothy must be a bold, creative pioneer, since he is one of the "ancients of the earth, and in the morning of the times."

Index